D1639706

(

London Jamaican

Real Language Series

General Editors:

Jennifer Coates, Roehampton Institute, London,
Jenny Cheshire, Universities of Fribourg and Neuchâtel, and
Euan Reid, Institute of Education, University of London

Titles published in the series:

David Lee Competing Discourses: Perspective and Ideology in Language
Norman Fairclough (Editor) Critical Language Awareness
James Milroy and Lesley Milroy (Editors) Real English: The Grammar of English Dialects in the British Isles
Mark Sebba London Jamaican: Language Systems in Interaction

London Jamaican:
Language Systems in Interaction

Mark Sebba

LONGMAN
London and New York

Longman Group UK Limited
Longman House, Burnt Mill,
Harlow, Essex CM20 2JE, England
and Associated Companies throughout the world.

Published in the United States of America by Longman Publishing,
New York

First published 1993

ISBN 0-582 08096-7 CSD
ISBN 0-582 08095-9 PPR

British Library Cataloguing-in-Publication Data
A catalogue record for this book is available from the British Library

Library of Congress Cataloging in Publication Data
Sebba, Mark.
  London Jamaican : Language systems in interaction / Mark Sebba.
  p. cm. – (Real language series)
  Includes bibliographical references and index.
  ISBN 0-582-08096-7. – ISBN 0-582-08095-9 (pbk.)
  1. English language–Dialects–Jamaica. 2. English language–
  Dialects–England–London. 3. Creole dialects, English–England–
  London. 4. Languages in contact–England–London. 5. Jamaicans–
  England–London–Language. 6. Creole dialects, English–Jamaica.
  7. Black English–England–London.   I. Title. II. Series.
  PE3313.S43   1993
  427'.97292--dc20   92-42560
                                                          CIP

Set by 7R in 10/12pt Sabon
Produced by Longman Singapore Publishers (Pte) Ltd.
Printed in Singapore

Contents

Acknowledgements

My thanks go, first and foremost to all who helped this research as informants: who took me, and more importantly, my tape recorder, into their homes and shared their conversations with me. Secondly, to those people – teachers, social workers and 'friends of friends', who helped me in various ways: finding informants, rooms to record in, places to stay and much else.

Let me record my thanks here to many people who have lent their intellectual powers to this research in one way or another: to Prof. R.B. Le Page, whose idea it was, who acted as Principal Investigator throughout the period of fieldwork; to Roger Hewitt, for help and encouragement; to Ben Rampton and the series editors, Jennifer Coates, Jenny Cheshire and Euan Reid for many helpful comments on the typescript. I appreciate their advice and any shortcomings are due to me entirely.

I am grateful, too, to the funders of the two research projects on which this book is based: the Nuffield Foundation for the initial small grant, and the Economic and Social Research Council for funding for a two-year period (Grant No. HR8682).

The time to write this book became available through the generosity of my colleagues in the Department of Linguistics, Lancaster University, who agreed to my having a term's sabbatical after only two years' service. My thanks to all of you.

Thanks are due, though inadequate to express my appreciation, to my wife, who has been married to this book (in its sickness and health) for well over a year. Thank you, Sharon, for your patience and support.

Transcription Conventions

(0.6)	Pause measured in seconds
x̰x̰x̰x̰	Laughter permeating segment
<laughter (1.4)>	Laughter, duration in seconds
xx ⌈ xxx ⌊ yyy	Speech in overlap
/, // etc.	Overlap/interruption (see note below)
=	'Latching' where the second speaker's talk follows that of the first without overlap or pause
: (also :: etc.)	Marker of length (vowel or consonant)
XYZ (capitals)	Increased loudness
(xxx)	Indistinct: brackets indicate uncertain transcription
* * *	Unintelligble speech: each * represents one syllable
yyy z̲z̲z̲ yyy	Underlined stretches are 'Creole' (see page 19)
%	Represents glottal stop (phonetically [ʔ]) (see page 158)

Note: For convenience of transcription not all overlaps are shown using long brackets. Shorter overlaps/interruptions are shown by / at the point of the first overlap, // at the point of the second, etc. For example,

A: I don' know / anything about it // you see
B: no
B: no
B: I see

could also be transcribed:

A: I don' know ⎡ anything about it ⎡ you see
B: ⎣ no   ⎣ no
B: I see

1 Introduction: Creole Comes to Britain

The Caribbean community in Britain is not a new arrival. Some British cities such as London, Cardiff, and Liverpool have long-established black communities[1]. Caribbeans who have come to Britain from abroad have probably always brought with them their own distinctively Caribbean varieties of language; yet it is only in the last two or three decades that educators and policy makers – and to some extent, the general public – have taken an interest in 'Black English' (also called Creole or Patois) in Britain.

Regrettably, much of this interest has had a negative focus. In education, the language of West Indians was (and to some extent still is) perceived as a problem (see Edwards 1979, 1982; Dalphinis 1991; and Chapter 9 of this book). During the 1960s and 1970s interest in the language of Caribbeans in British schools led eventually to the publication of specialised teaching materials and the implementation of policies in the light of two Commissions of Inquiry (Bullock 1975; Rampton 1981).

In spite of this, the quantity of research on Caribbean language in Britain is not large. Furthermore, since there are now well-established Caribbean communities in a dozen or so English cities, each with a slightly different population distribution and distinct needs, any attempt to discuss the language behaviour of Caribbeans in Britain will need to consider each community separately. This book is mainly about research carried out in London – home of Britain's largest Caribbean community, though not necessarily typical of all the Caribbean communities in Britain.

The linguistic roots of the British Caribbean community obviously lie in the Caribbean. So before going on to explain the origins of the London-based research, I shall give some background to the language situation in the Caribbean.

'Creole' and 'Standard English' in the Caribbean

The Caribbean – even if we restrict our focus of interest to the formerly British parts – is not linguistically homogeneous. However, the ex-British Caribbean territories share enough of their social and linguistic history to allow us to call them, for some purposes, a single language community.

In each territory, Standard English is an official language and a language of education, at least in the current phase of that territory's history. In fact, the length of time that Standard English has had this status differs widely from place to place: over three hundred years in Jamaica, less than two hundred in Dominica. In all cases, however, Standard English has been present for long enough to have had a substantial impact on the language practices of the communities in question.

In the parts of the Caribbean under consideration, at the same time as Standard English is used in the official and public domains, a local *creole* language is the language of everyday interaction for the majority of the population. Creoles have been a focus of interest for linguists for over a century, because of their distinctive history. In linguistics, 'creole' is a technical term referring to a class of languages which originate through contact between two or more already existing languages. Creoles generally arise through a prior *pidgin* stage. Regular or prolonged contact between two groups who speak mutually unintelligible languages may result in the formation of a pidgin – a language which is nobody's native language but serves as a means of communication for a limited range of purposes related to the contact situation. Usually, pidgins derive most of their vocabulary from one language (the *lexifier*), while their grammar is derived from the various 'input' languages (including the lexifier) on the one hand, and on the other, from universal tendencies of human beings to simplify their native languages in order to make them more intelligible to foreigners.[2]

In the West African slave trade, a pidgin form of English (i.e. a pidgin with English as lexifier) was used for communication between the English slavers and their African counterparts, as well as among those Africans involved in the trade who did not have any other language in common. Pidgins with other European lexifiers (Portuguese, Spanish and Dutch) also developed as a result of this trade. These pidgin languages were also learnt by the slaves themselves, before, during or after their passage across the Atlantic to the Americas. The slaves themselves needed the pidgin as a lingua franca, not just for communication with their captors, but to communicate among themselves; a typical cargo would bring together slaves from many language groups, and on arrival in the American ports, they were deliberately split up to reduce the likelihood of conspiracies.

The transition from a *pidgin* to a *creole* language takes place when the pidgin becomes a native language for some of its speakers. This will occur once a pidgin-speaking community is sufficiently settled for children to be born, and to grow up hearing the pidgin spoken all around them. In the case of the Caribbean slave communities, this probably took only a short time: for example, we know that the emergence of Sranan Tongo, an English-lexified Creole spoken in the coastal region of Surinam, can be dated with reasonable accuracy to a period between the arrival of the first English slave-owning planters in the middle of the seventeenth century, and their expulsion by the Dutch: a total of less than thirty years. Once established as the most widely spoken language in the community, the Creole would soon supersede African languages for most functions except, perhaps, religious ones. Today, although there is a definite legacy of African languages in many parts of the Caribbean, the languages themselves are no longer spoken there.

The origins of the Caribbean Creole languages in slavery and plantation labour have ensured that they have never enjoyed high status in their own communities – notwithstanding various local attempts over the last century, mainly by intellectuals without government support, to raise their status. The existence of a *diglossic* relationship (Ferguson 1959; Fishman 1965, 1967) – a strict division in terms of function and status – between Standard English (the 'high' variety) and the local Creole language (the 'low' variety), is the norm in most places where a Creole is used.

The above description hides a significant division among the ex-British Caribbean territories, for while in most of these a Creolised variety of English is spoken, there are several – Dominica and St Lucia being the best known – where a Creolised variety of French, a language known as Kwéyòl, is the vernacular. A French-lexified Creole is, or has been in common use in several other territories as well – Trinidad, Grenada and St Vincent among them. Thus although the sociolinguistic profile 'High: Standard English/Low: Creole' holds good throughout the ex-British Caribbean almost without exception, we need to make a distinction between those places where the majority speak a Creole with English-derived vocabulary, and those where most or some of the populace speak a Creole with French-derived vocabulary.

In much of this book, the Creolised varieties of French will be left out of the discussion. This is not because they lack interest, or are unrepresented in Britain: neither of these is true. However, in numerical terms their communities in Britain are small, so that their linguistic influence on the Afro-Caribbean community construed as a whole is weak. That is one reason: another is that substantial ethnographic research on speakers of French Creole in Britain has up until now been virtually non-existent, so that there is little to report.

London Jamaican 'discovered'

By the 1970s, the 'West Indian language problem' had been probed and discussed by educators and policy makers, but still rather little actual research had been done on the language of the Caribbeans. Caribbeans were settled in many parts of Britain; in London, they were a substantial proportion of the population in several boroughs.[3] Probably Brixton is the most famous of the London 'Caribbean' areas, but there are several others with a substantial Afro-Caribbean population, such as Lewisham, Deptford, New Cross, Leyton and Harlesden.

In schools in these areas and other parts of London, children whose native language was a Caribbean Creole had been in evidence since the 1950s. Now, however, a new phenomenon was noticed. In 1980 Rosen and Burgess wrote in their book, *Languages and Dialects of London School Children*:

> At the centre of the complexity introduced in London classrooms by the presence of overseas dialects of English, lies what we have called London/Jamaican – a magnetic, political, social and peer

group dialect for Eastern as well as Western Caribbean pupils and to some extent for West African and even white London speakers too. The central point is that the range of different patois spoken reflects both the complexity of the linguistic situation in the Caribbean and also the modifications to these being made by children growing up within the overseas speech communities in London. (Rosen and Burgess 1980: 58)

Attempting to find out about the extent to which Creole was used by London schoolchildren, Rosen and Burgess asked teachers to specify whether pupils spoke '(a) Standard, (b) a full regional Creole, or (c) a London/regional mix' (1980: 58). The authors say that they are 'aware that all such information must be interpreted as indicative rather than hard and fast' (p. 58): such caution is certainly necessary. Very few teachers are qualified to make assessments on the basis of linguistic criteria, and Rosen and Burgess's categories were in themselves vague enough to be interpreted differently by different teachers. Because we know that most British-born Caribbeans use a language mixing mode for informal interactions, using elements of both Creole and British English, the odds are in favour of any one child being put into the 'London/regional mix' category. This is just what Rosen and Burgess's figures show for the Jamaican pupils they studied. Of 507, 52 were reported to speak 'a full Creole', 11 'standard', 444 (88 per cent) 'London/overseas dialect'. Their figures for the Eastern Caribbean are less clear cut (also predictable as Barbadian Creole is itself less distant from Standard English than Jamaican), but do show a tendency for teachers to categorise them as 'mixed' speakers. This kind of gross categorisation really tells us nothing about how the language varieties are 'mixed' – neither the kind of mixing nor the proportions.

Unfortunately, the moment of London Jamaican's emergence passed undocumented either by historians or linguists, but anecdotal evidence points to its being a phenomenon which developed in the early 1970s. Some even go so far as to link its emergence to the coming of reggae music to Britain, *circa* 1970, and the first reggae film widely seen in Britain, Perry Henzell's (1972) *The Harder They Come* starring Jimmy Cliff. It is likely that the phenomenon of *white* Creole use owes much to the popularisation of Jamaican musical styles, but the role of music in promoting Creole among the Caribbean population is harder to assess (see next section).[4]

The Jamaican and British varieties of Jamaican Creole are in a dynamic relationship. According to Dalphinis (1991: 49), 'Contact between Britain and the Caribbean is extensive, and growing'. There is a considerable movement of young blacks between the West Indies and Britain. Many have spent as much as several years there being raised by grandparents. Others have spent long summer holidays there. Even where individuals have not been to the West Indies themselves, they often live in a household with an older person of the same generation (e.g. an older sibling) who either was born there or has spent some time there. The Caribbean (particularly Jamaican) influence on the British Creole is thus continually being renewed. In addition there is now some use of Creole varieties in the British media: in films such as *The Harder They Come, Babylon* (directed by Franco Rosso, Great Britain, 1980) and *Countryman*, (directed by Dick Jobson, Great Britain, 1982). The advent of Channel 4 in 1982 provided a space for more minority-orientated programmes than previously: Caribbean accents and occasional use of Creole have been regular features of situation comedies such as *No Problem* in the early 1980s and *Desmonds* in the late 1980s to early 1990s.

Creole-language culture in Britain: Rastafari, Reggae and Toasting

There can be no doubt that Creole, in particular Jamaican Creole, derives much of its attraction for the youth from its association with certain forms of culture. Three of these in particular – Rastafarianism, variously defined as a 'religion' or as a 'movement' (Gilroy 1987: 187), reggae, and toasting – can be seen as significant not only in providing a centre of attraction towards Creole-based culture for black (and some white) youth at various times, but also in providing access to and models of Jamaican Creole through social networks and relatively high media profiles.

Rastafari

Rastafarianism has many followers in London. Rastafarian speech is probably best described as a variety of Jamaican Creole with special lexis and morphology. To date there are no published linguistic descriptions of language in any Rastafarian community, apart from descriptions by Pollard (1980, 1983, 1984a, 1984b).

Ryan (1980) is an unpublished description of linguistic aspects of a Rastafarian community in the West Midlands. A study by Bones (1986a) is the work of a non-linguist with a social sciences background. As a Rastafarian, he has an insider's knowledge of the language, though many of his claims would not be accepted by linguists: for example, 'as a language Afro-Lingua [Rastafarian Creole] does not need grammar and rules because it relies on improvisation, quickwittedness and skill at manipulating words' (1986a: 49). Bones stresses the importance of language in the Rastafarian religious culture: 'according to Rasta doctrine and reasoning, a language must have great significance in terms of its words, sounds and "powah", which means "power" . . . the "powah" is what gives Rasta strength and makes him formidable' (1986a: 48–9). Bones thus describes the effect of Rastafarian speech on Jamaican attitudes: 'Those Jamaicans who were not Rastas were somewhat ashamed of Patois. They spoke it only because they were unable to do "better". But the Rastas felt that the language was the African people's own, that they should be proud of it and should set about improving it' (1986a: 44). Hence, 'the Rastafarians of Britain are genuinely proud of Afro-Lingua. The young black people of Britain who are into black consciousness and cultural awareness are keen to speak Afro-Lingua because it reinforces their awareness and gives them hope where otherwise there would be despair' (1986a: 44–5).

Although some of the distinctive lexis of the London variety of Jamaican Creole may have its origins in Rasta speech, there is no clear evidence that Rastafarian influence on the *structure* of the Creole goes any further than that. However, the positive attitudes of Rastafarians towards Creole – in contrast to the negative attitudes of the Caribbean establishment, the majority of older generation Caribbeans in Britain, and the white British establishment – may well have had the effect of promoting the use of Creole among black (and to some extent, white) youth. In the absence of any research findings, it is impossible to be sure about this, let alone quantify it.

Among Afro-Caribbean adolescents in the early 1980s the Rasta image was a popular one, especially for boys, many of whom dressed as Rastas and affected Rasta styles of speech. Probably only a minority of these carried the commitment through into adulthood, though as Gilroy writes (1987: 187), 'by looking at the broad and diverse use to which the language and symbols of Rastafari have been put, it is possible to conceive it as a movement in which the lines dividing different levels of commitment are necessarily flexible'. At the time this study was carried out, the influence of Rastafari (and with it, reggae) was already in decline, victim of political changes in the Caribbean and the United States and the ascendancy of new cultural styles. 'The interpretive community formed around Rasta language and symbols, presided over and tutored in dread ethics by Marley and other outernational reggae artists, simply could not withstand these changes. Its cultural and political hegemony began to dissolve' (Gilroy 1987: 190).

Reggae

Reggae music in the 1970s and 1980s popularised Caribbean speech among non-Caribbean youth, not only in Britain but in many other countries. However, its linguistic significance for the Caribbean community in Britain is less clear. Some black children may have had their first experience of Jamaican Creole from reggae lyrics, while others may have been attracted to Creole for the first time because of the music. Reggae music and Creole are closely associated, cf. Bones (1986b: 55): 'For reggae, most definitely, the music and the language are one and the same thing. The message can't be different because it's one sound, one word and one mouth, people, culture and all else that related to the people of reggae and Afro-Lingua.' However, not all reggae lyrics are in Creole. Bob Marley, a Rastafarian reggae musician idolised by millions of all races, sang many of his lyrics in something much closer to Jamaican-accented Standard English than broad Jamaican Creole. For this reason, I can agree only cautiously with Bones (1986b: 66) who writes: 'In my view, reggae music, and especially the deejaying aspect of the music, has established itself, without any doubt at all, as the principal transmitter of the Jamaican language (Afro-lingua).'

Toasting

The 'deejaying aspect of the music' mentioned by Bones is the basis of another art form, 'toasting' or the public recitation of metric, rhyming verse. In Britain's largely black discos and dancehalls, which have always been dependent on mainly recorded music, the role of the DJ or Master of Ceremonies was able to take on a special significance. The DJ provided a link between the music and the audience and his or her commentary on the music became an integral part of the performance, which often involved a variety of other 'special effects' such as 'scratching' the records, playing more than one at a time, and so on. From its origins as comment and interpretation of recorded music, 'toasting' evolved into an event in its own right, giving the DJ an opportunity to display verbal 'improvisation, quickwittedness and skill' in Bones's words, and in addition to provide a 'politically engaged comment' (Gilroy 1987: 193) in many cases.[5]

As well as toasting, the 'dubbing' of poetry to an instrumental background became popular in the late 1970s to early 1980s. Probably the most famous exponent of this art is Linton Kwesi Johnson. His poems are also published in book form using English-based orthography. Many of them are in Jamaican Creole, mixed to varying degrees with English.

It seems that Rastafari, reggae and toasting may have been crucial in asserting the cultural dominance of the Jamaican element within the Caribbean community in Britain. This cultural ascendancy of the Jamaicans (cf. Bones 1986b) would help account for the existence of 'London Jamaican' when there is no 'London Bajan', 'London Trinidadian' or 'London Guyanese'. Rosen and Burgess noted that 'London/Jamaican' was a magnet 'for Eastern as well as Western Caribbean pupils' (1980: 58). Numerically the Jamaicans form the majority of the Caribbean community in most parts of London as well as other large centres; yet even where they do not, it is *Jamaican* which provides a focus for the Creole of black youth. An outstanding example of this is given in Tate's (1984) study of a group of Rastafarians of Dominican descent in Bradford. Approximately two-thirds of Bradford's 3000 Caribbeans are Dominican by birth or descent, from French Patois-speaking homes. Yet Tate, herself a Jamaican, found that her second-generation informants used Jamaican Creole as their in-group language, and sounded so authentic that they could pass for Jamaicans in Jamaica, in her judgement (personal communication).

The 'London Jamaican' Research Project

In the early 1980s, there were reports of widespread use of 'Jamaican Creole' among Caribbean children in London schools, but little was actually known about it. Rosen and Burgess (1980) had remarked on the existence of 'London/Jamaican'. Somewhat later, V.K. Edwards noted that:

> D'Costa (1981), herself a Jamaican, considered on the basis of a visit to Britain that Jamaican Creole is spreading 'as an identifying group dialect common to all West Indians' but does not document her claim. We are clearly not yet in a position to state confidently whether a distinctly British variety of West Indian Creole has emerged, whether there is any geographical variation within Britain, or whether the various island differences continue to exert an influence on the language of second and third generation West Indians. (Edwards 1982: 2)

What Rosen and Burgess had called 'London/Jamaican' begged description: so far, there were no clear accounts of what it was like. Though both Rosen and Burgess and D'Costa had identified this language variety of black adolescents with *Jamaican* specifically, in the absence of a description, no one really knew whether it had the features of Jamaican Creole or not. Was it an altogether new variety of Creole? Was it *really* based on Jamaican? What was its relationship with London English for those who spoke it? And who actually *were* its speakers – adolescents or preadolescents? Of Jamaican origin exclusively, or not?

These are the questions which I sought to answer through my fieldwork which began in November, 1981, as part of two research projects based at the University of York. Both were headed by Prof. R.B. Le Page, who had produced some of the first linguistic studies of Jamaican Creole about twenty years previously (Le Page 1961; Le Page and De Camp 1960; Cassidy and Le Page 1980, originally published 1967). The first of these projects (lasting one year) was supported by a grant from the Nuffield Foundation and the second (for two years) by the Economic and Social Research Council. Altogether, fieldwork lasted from about October 1981 to mid-1984.

In the initial phase of my fieldwork, my contacts were made through schools in the areas of Leytonstone (in the borough of

Waltham Forest) and Catford (which at that time was in the area of the Inner London Education Authority, now abolished). Most of the fieldwork consisted of making tape recordings of pupils from different age groups: often I left them alone, in pairs, with a request to 'talk black' or 'chat Patois'. This technique produced a great deal of interesting material, but I still felt a need to achieve more insight into the language behaviour of my informants – especially outside school. I was very fortunate to find a number of people, in their late teens and early twenties, who were willing to take a tape recorder home with them and make recordings of themselves, their families and their friends in conversation. It is these that make up the greater part of the transcribed conversations in Appendix 2 of this book.

Reference points in Jamaican and British English

In the next chapter, I will give some examples of 'Jamaican' which I collected from children and adolescents in London. One of the questions which must be answered is whether these do indeed show the predominant influence of *Jamaican* Creole or whether they are better described in terms of some other variety. I will discuss this question in detail in Chapter 4. In the meantime, however, it is necessary to have some 'reference points', some guidelines for distinguishing the different varieties which have influenced, or *may* have influenced, the language of these young speakers.

For our purposes, it will be enough to have a general idea of what distinguishes the Caribbean Creoles from the varieties of British English to which second-generation Caribbeans in London have been exposed. For both a practical and a theoretical reason I shall concentrate on describing those influences in terms of just *four* varieties: Standard British English, London English (henceforth LE), Jamaican Standard English and Jamaican Creole (henceforth JC), with emphasis on just two of these, LE and JC.

The practical reason is that of all the Caribbean Creoles, Jamaican is that which has been best and most accessibly described. (Unfortunately such good descriptions do not exist for LE!) Earlier in this chapter I gave some idea of the linguistic complexities of the Caribbean. I could not hope to set out details of all the Caribbean varieties which *might* have a role in shaping the linguistic behaviour of young Caribbeans in London. Describing just JC is a reasonable compromise, especially as the points of difference between the idealised 'broadest' JC and other 'broad' English-lexicon creoles of the Caribbean are not great. All share many rules of grammar and phonology. There are relatively minor differences which I shall point out where they become relevant.

The theoretical reason for using Jamaican as a reference point is that, as I shall argue in Chapter 4, the main Creole influence on 'London Jamaican' (henceforth LJ) really *is* Jamaican; the comparison is therefore the appropriate one to make.

Appendix 1 of this book provides a partial contrastive grammar of Caribbean Creoles (with emphasis on Jamaican) on the one hand, and LE (with some references to Standard English/R.P.) on the other. Only those features of grammar and phonology which are *contrastive* – in other words, which are useful for determining whether what we are hearing at any particular moment is Jamaican Standard, JC, Standard English or LE – have been discussed. Fuller descriptions of these varieties are available elsewhere. Each key contrastive feature of grammar or phonology has been given a number in brackets ([F 1], [G 1], etc.) and these will be used elsewhere in the book when reference is made to these specific features of the language varieties in contact.

Notes

1. The black population of London was estimated at between fourteen and twenty thousand in the eighteenth century, or 2.2 per cent of the total (Alexander and Dewjee 1981). During the period of the slave trade and plantation labour in the West Indies, a certain number of black Caribbeans found their way to Britain, frequently as sailors or as slaves or servants accompanying their masters. During the nineteenth century their numbers declined, due to intermarriage and emigration (for example, several hundred went to Sierra Leone in 1787: Henderson 1960.) During the First World War, several thousand black labourers were brought to Britain, once again boosting the small black community. However, it was not until after the Second World War that immigration from the West Indies began to reach significant numbers. According to census returns, there were 15 000 persons born in the West Indies living in England and Wales in 1951, of whom 6 500 were born in Jamaica. By the end of 1958, an estimated 117 000 West Indians had entered Britain (Wood

1960). The 1981 Census reports list 295 179 persons born in the Caribbean as being normally resident in Great Britain, or 0.55 per cent of the total population of 53 556 911. In 1962 the Commonwealth Immigrants Act came into effect: its object was to limit immigration from the New Commonwealth, including the West Indies. From that time onward the flow of migrants from the West Indies to Britain has declined steadily: recently there seems to have been a net outflow. However, the Afro-Caribbean communities themselves have continued to grow, as the migrants of the first generation have settled and had families of their own.

2. There is space here only to summarise very briefly the large amount of research on pidgin and Creole languages. For more detailed discussion see e.g. Mühlhäusler 1986, Romaine 1988, Todd 1990; also Le Page and Tabouret-Keller 1985 on Creoles in particular.

3. In some cities, certain areas, such as Toxteth in Liverpool, Moss Side in Manchester, and Brixton in London have become known as 'black areas' in popular perception. It is difficult even to guess at the actual figures, but probably even in these areas thought of as 'largely black' less than half the population is Caribbean. The Caribbean population has been 'ghettoised' (though not on the American model, since they remain a minority even in the 'ghetto' areas) for a variety of reasons, among them discrimination in housing by Local Authorities, estate agents and private landlords: economic factors; and the desire to live with other black people for the sake of community, solidarity and protection against racist attacks.

4. However, there is circumstantial evidence which suggests that the date 1972 may well be close. Children of primary school age seem to make only limited use of Creole. Informal observations suggest that it first becomes popular as a peer group language at the age of eleven or twelve. By the first year of secondary school, most Caribbean children in areas of reasonably high Caribbean settlement are speaking it to some extent at least. The Commonwealth Immigrants Act came into force in 1962; hence from that time onward, the proportion of British-born Caribbeans out of the total Caribbean population of Britain began to rise considerably. If the first British-born generation of Caribbeans can be said to date from the period around 1960, then it began to reach its Creole-speaking adolescence around 1972 – as a result of a coincidence of factors which may or may not have something to do with the popularity of Jamaican music around that time.

5. For more detail on toasting and some examples, see the discussions in Hewitt (1986: 114ff) or Gilroy (1987: 192ff).

2 In search of 'London Jamaican'

Two 'Creole' Stories

Susan, a twelve year-old girl in an East London school told the following story:

Extract 1: The ghost

> One day me met a witch Jamaica [inaudible] me (gorra) mother –
> me saw her dere, me sit down an she tell me all the story alrigh%?
> One story was about the ghost she see – this is the story whe she
> tell me wha% she see, alright. She, one day she tell me dat she saw
> a ghost – or somefing like a ghost, a person who come in the
> house – she tell me she pick up a brick and break i bones – de ting
> run like she no know what.

The spelling, even modified to show some of the most striking features of Susan's speech, does little to convey its true flavour. Even so, the transcription reveals some obvious grammatical and phonological features of Jamaican Creole (JC). (In the following discussion, I refer to specific grammatical and phonological features of JC and London English (LE) using numbers in square brackets. See Appendix 1 for a detailed explanation of each of these. Other transcription conventions, such as the use of '%' for a glottal stop, are explained on page ix.) Susan uses *me* for the first person pronoun [G2], and unmarked past tense [G4] in *tell, see, pick* and *run*, and she has initial /t/ in *ting*, 'thing' [P17]. There are many other Jamaican phonological features in Susan's speech which are not shown in the transcription above, for example, the pronunciation of the vowels of *day, all, story, ghost, break* and *bones* [P4,P5,P6] and the presence of postvocalic /r/ in *person* [P15].

However, Susan also uses several distinctively LE features in telling her story. Only two of these, /f/ in *somefing* [P17] and the glottalling of /t/ in *alright* and *what* [P19], are shown in the transcription, but there are several others: the vowel of *come, one, up* and *run* [P3]; and the vocalisation of /l/ in the second two cases of *tell me* [P16], which contrast with a clear /l/ in the other instances of *tell*. The use of *saw* instead of *see* for the past tense indicates British English or JE rather than JC [G4].

There are some other features of the language of this story which need some comment. For example, while the /r/ of *person* is pronounced (as it would be in JC) [P15], the speaker has also pronounced /r/ in *mother*, where it is less usual for Jamaicans to pronounce it, and at the end of *Jamaica*, where it does not occur historically at all. Her pronunciation of the diphthong in *down, about* and *house* is not like JC or LE: it is closest to RP [P9].

The speaker who told the story above is a twelve year-old white girl, born in London to white British-born parents. She has never been to the Caribbean in her life, but most of her friends are black British: to their companionship she owes her aptitude for talking Creole. Creole use by white adolescents and others is a well-known phenomenon, thoroughly documented by Roger Hewitt in his book *White Talk Black Talk* (Hewitt 1986), so finding a white girl who can 'talk Black' is not in itself surprising. Still, it is instructive to look at how she has constructed this form of speech approximating to JC, and with what degree of success.

From the comparison I have made above of features of her speech with those of JC and LE, it is apparent that in linguistic terms, she has hit her target some of the time, but not all of it. She is rather good at 'doing' Jamaican vowels, except for the vowel of STRUT [P3], which always comes out as the LE version. She has clear /l/ twice – a Jamaican would be expected to have it everywhere – yet twice she has vocalisation of /l/ as in LE. She has JC /t/ for the initial consonant of *thing*, but in *something*, she has the LE variant /f/ (JC usually has *sinting*). While she has /r/ in *person* where it should be in JC, she has pronounced /r/ at the end of *mother*, where Jamaicans usually do not pronounce it, and at the end of *Jamaica*, where historically it is absent: in this last case displaying the type of hypercorrection for which John F.

Kennedy (a speaker of the r-less Boston English) was famous. Although she uses the base form of the verb to indicate past tense as in JC, she does not do it consistently: she also uses several morphologically distinct past tense forms.

To the linguist, it is clear at once that she has not *really* managed to speak JC, she has just made an imitation of it which might fool people not really familiar with that language. No *real* Jamaican, one might feel, would be fooled by this. Nevertheless, in a 'matched guise' test which I administered to a class of fourteen to fifteen year-old adolescents in the speaker's own home area, seven out of eleven black pupils judged her to be black on the basis of an extract from the story above (see Chapter 4 for a discussion).

Stephen, a boy of about sixteen in a school not far from Susan's, told me the following story:

Extract 2: Sounds are for big people

Me was trodding down de road and me come across me bredder 'e – me ask 'im for some money an 'e say 'e na got. An' 'e say 'Wha% you wan% a money for?' Me say me wan% go, you know, listen to some sound, and then 'e say 'you cyaan go sound, you too young to go sound' I say 'Wha you mean by that?' 'Im say that er, you know sound it a sort t'ing for big people cause when me get stab up whe me go say, me mudder go star% argue wiv me, because when most of the time when you go sound you know trouble an' all that does arise. So me say all me want is a poun' to get in [inaudible] and me ten pence bus fare. 'Im say 'alrigh% den, trod along dereso bu% if you come back wiv a knife in your back don', y'know, [inaudible] come an' complain to me.' So me went down dere an' me called for me spar dem and 'im come along wiv me and 'e . . . an' 'e check some woman down there, y'know check some skirt – jus' grind up some daughter y'know, smoke weed an' t'ing.

Again, this narrative shows both Creole and LE features. Unlike the previous passage, this one has several vocabulary items specific to (originally) black youth culture, for example *bredder* (brother – in the community rather than biological sense), *sound* (a large mobile disco – but see Gilroy 1987: 164ff for a fuller description), *spar* (friend), *skirt* and *daughter* (both words for women), while other words like *trod* and *check* are not used in a Standard English way. Specifically Creole features of the grammar include the subject pronouns *me* and *'im* [G2], use of the negator *no* (na) in line 2 [G15], omission of infinitive marker *to* after *want* (l.3) and *start* (l.6)[G18], lack of past tense marking on *say* and *check*, *grind* and *smoke* [G4], and the plural marker *dem* in *spar-dem* [G9]. Creole features of the phonology include the pronunciation of the vowels of *some* [P3], *sound* [P9], *sort* [P11], *back* [P2] (*wiv a knife in your back*), *come* (*come along wiv me*) [P3], *daughter* [P4,P13]; *skirt* and *fare* (with /r/)[P15]; *thing* as /ting/, and *mother* as /mada/ [P17]; and the distinctively short open vowels in *say* [sɛ] [P5] and *go* [gɒ] [P6].

However, as in the first passage, there are also many identifiably London features: in the grammar, many of the forms of the verbs (*was trodding, called, went, was*) [G4-G6]; in the phonology, the vowel sounds of *down* [P9], *across* [P1], *want* [P1], *along* [P1], *called* [P11]; the glottalling of /t/ in *what, want, start, but* [P19]; and /v/ in *with* (/wiv/) twice [P17]. The MOUTH vowel [P9] is especially interesting because it shows all the possible variants, from the extreme basilectal variant which occurs before /n/ in *sound* [sɒŋ] through the JC/JE variant [sɔʊn] and [pɔʊn], something close to RP in *down* [daʊn] to the Cockney variant in [dæ:n] twice. We noticed that the first speaker, Susan did not use the JC vowel in STRUT words [P3]. Stephen is inconsistent, using the JC form rarely (in *bus, some* and *come*, each only once) but usually having the Cockney variant (in *come, money, young, mother, trouble, does, just* and *up*).

So Stephen's narrative is comparable to Susan's, in showing a high degree of grammatical and phonological similarity to JC, while at the same time showing distinctively LE features, with a fair amount of inconsistency.

Stephen is a boy of mixed Jamaican and St Vincentian parentage, born and raised only a few miles away from the white girl who provided the first narrative. Unlike many of my black informants, this boy had actually lived in the Caribbean for five years: between the ages of three and six in his mother's country, Jamaica, and later, when he was of school age, for two years in St Vincent. In fact, his speech reveals one or two features which may be due to St Vincentian influence: in particular, the use of *does* in *trouble . . . does arise*. This use of *does* (actually an invariant preverbal particle /dɒz/) to indicate habitual/usual actions is characteristic of St Vincentian but not of JC.

What are we to make of the similarities between these two speakers, one white, the other black? I am not suggesting that white children or adolescents are generally as good at speaking Creole as black children. Nor am I suggesting that black children are somehow linguistically deficient or unable to separate English from Creole. Rather, many speakers 'construct' the language they variously call Creole, Patois, black talk, bad talk or Jamaican on the basis of a collection of stereotypical features which are associated with JC as spoken in Jamaica. The relatively frequent mis-matches between speakers' 'Patois' and the presumed model (JC) indicate that for those speakers, 'Patois' does not come as naturally as LE.

This means that for many of its black speakers as well as virtually all its white speakers, the London variety of Creole is something like a second language or dialect, learnt around the time of transition between childhood and adolescence. While this may not be true for some black speakers, particularly in neighbourhoods with a high proportion of Caribbeans, it seems to be true for the majority of my black informants from the areas of Leyton, Catford and Southwark.

'Chattin' Patois' and 'plain English'

Most of the young black people in my study use LE most of the time, even when speaking to other members of the family who were born in the Caribbean. For them, the uses of Creole are quite restricted: it is always used in conjunction with British English (usually LE) in a code-switching style, and has a limited set of functions. Nearly all these individuals are fully competent native speakers of British English, so they do not actually require Creole for strictly *communicative* purposes; for them, Creole fulfils a number of other roles mostly related to its symbolic significance as a marker of black identity.

At this point we need to separate out two different activities which can easily be confused. To the linguist interested only in the *form* of language, 'speaking Creole' may mean using identifiably Creole grammar, phonology and lexis, as, for example, B.L. Bailey's Jamaican informants did when providing her with examples of JC for her book, *Jamaican Creole Syntax* (1966). By contrast, in London 'talking black' or 'chatting Patois' can be seen as a social act where speakers, coming to the conversation with similar models of the stereotyped 'Creole', but different degrees of competence in it and different amounts of motivation, negotiate a language which they agree is 'Patois'/'Creole'/'black talk' etc. Each party to the conversation uses as many 'Creole' tokens as s/he feels comfortable with. That the result is regarded as 'Creole', 'Patois' etc. by the speakers is the result of a social rather than a linguistic process, in which two 'opposing' codes, 'ordinary English' (i.e. British English, usually LE) and 'Patois' are construed to exist in the repertoire of speakers. Thus two speakers who normally use hardly any Creole forms might feel they were 'chatting Patois' when they were actually using fewer Creole tokens than two heavy Creole users who felt they were speaking 'ordinary English.'

If talking Patois is best analysed as a social activity rather than a purely *informational* one, then the narratives by Susan and Stephen can be said to be exceptional in that they do not involve any other participants from the same speech community. Though they were spoken for my benefit, I could not be assumed to share the same norms. In the rest of this book, the emphasis will be on studying conversation, since it is only in conversation that the 'negotiated' nature of Creole usage can come to light.

Let us now look at one conversation and see how this works. The speakers here are Joan and Carol, two fifteen year-old girls, both of Jamaican parentage, who attend a school in Catford, London SE6. (Note that here and elsewhere in the book, underlined stretches of talk mean that it is phonologically and/or grammatically marked as 'Creole'.)

Extract 3: Catford Girls' Possee

1	J	did you go to Jackie's par%y?
		(1.0)
	C	who Jackie <u>Lomax</u>
	J	yeah
	C	<u>no one never invi%e me</u>
5	J	I heard that she had a really nice par%y an' Cheryl
		said there was a lo% of boys there (0.6) you know
		and they (were) playin' pass the parcel an' that
	C	is it?
		yeah
10	C	<u>she invite you?</u>

```
        J    no
        C    she never invite me neither an Leonie 'ave one as
             well never invite never tell me not'in' (0.4) me no
             business too!
        J    Leonie have party?!
 15     C    man (1.0) Leonie have party (0.4) when? (1.2)
             don' remember when it was but she did tell all o' dem
             no fi- t say not'in' (0.6) cau' she no wan' too much
             Cyatford gyal de dere (1.0) an' Jackie 'ave one too
             (0.4) never say not'in'
 20     J    yeah Jackie's one was only meant to – meant to – meant
             to be for abou% (.) ten gels (0.6) you know, get-togevver
             part%y sor% of fing (0.2) but I heard that
             the G-Fours Possee did go 'n' quite a lo% of
             uvver people did go
 25     C    me no business (1.0) 'im never say not'in' to me about i
             (0.4) an' every day me see ('im) (0.4) 'im never
             say not'in' so me no care (2.0) don' really business
             (but) yeah, cause it was on the fifteenth innit (0.4)
             that time I was goin' out (to the) Bouncing Ball so (.)
 30          even if she did invite me me wouldn't a go
             (1.4)
        J    m:
        C    and we see, um, before we went we see, um (0.8) what was
             de flim called (de) m Private Lessons (0.8) film is rubbish man!
 35          No dutty part no ina it but em – dem a put i at – put it as X
             (1.0)
        J    Yeah I see them advertise it I thought it would be somethin'
             really great y'know but lo% of people from my class went an'
             see it but them say it was rubbish
 40     C    'course man, 'course they were showin' it last night in school
             as well
        J    they show Private Lessons in school yesterday?
        C    yeah, video club you know de video club yeah
        J    is it?
 45     C    m::
        J    I never did hear nuffing about that you know
        C    yeah (0.6) and when I went to see it right all o' dem
             was saying say it's supposed to teach you what the school don'
             teach you me no see not'in' ina dat whe school no teach you (0.6)
 50          lot o' rubbish (0.2) it coulda jus' be A an' done
        J    nye::ah (.) 'cause everybody goin' to see dat 'cause dem
             advertise it so great innit
        C    you know wh' I mean (0.8) load o' rubbish really
```

Let us take a close look now at what actually happens in this conversation. These girls had actually been *requested* to have a conversation in 'Jamaican', and had said that they would do so. Of course, it is unusual to be asked to have a conversation in a particular language; in fact, it is unusual to be asked to have a conversation in the presence of a tape recorder at all. This may have had an effect on the conversation: first, in respect of the content, which may have been different from what they would otherwise have talked about, and secondly in that the girls may have tried consciously to use 'Jamaican'. If the latter were the case, then we might expect there to be a lot of Creole forms in the speech of both girls.

However, looking at the underlined stretches, which are those showing one or more grammatical, lexical or phonological features of Creole origin, it is apparent that Carol uses far more creole forms than Joan. Right from the very beginning of this extract, where Joan poses a question in LE, and receives a response from Carol which uses Creole vowels in the pronunciation of the surname Lomax, there is a pattern of Carol using more Creole than Joan. Carol's speech shows Creole features in almost every turn. Overall, Joan's only uses a few Creole features: some Creole past tense forms (*did go*, etc. [G4,G7]); use of *them/dem* as a subject pronoun (*dem advertise it*, etc; and some Creole vowels (*great* = [gɹɛt], [P5]) and intonation in questions ('*Leonie have party?*'). By contrast, Carol uses a wide variety of Creole features, grammatical, lexical and phonological.

That Joan uses less Creole than Carol should not obscure the fact that in the course of the conversation, Joan accommodates to Carol by using increasingly more Creole features. For her first three turns, including one rather long turn (ll. 5–7) Joan uses no Creole features; finally at l.14 she asks, using Creole intonation, '*Leonie have party?*'. From this point onward, all of Joan's turns (except for the very short ones of the 'm-hm' variety) show at least one identifiably Creole feature. Joan can be said to be responding to Carol's relatively heavy use of Creole by increasing the 'Creole feature rating' of her own utterances: thus the two 'negotiate a language' which is identifiable as 'Creole' or 'Patois' by virtue of there being Creole features in the speech of all parties, though to differing degrees.

Joan's use of Creole is so limited that it might be called token-istic. Is it then restricted to ritual, stereotypical or culturally sym-bolic forms? Many Creole users, both black and white, evoke a 'black stereotype' by sprinkling their speech with a few Creol-isms, but these are nearly always lexical – tags like *man, guy, star, spar, y'know*, or *cho*, or swear words like *raas, turaatid, bom-boklaat*. (See Hewitt 1986: 135ff. for a description of the 'cultur-al' mode of Creole use mainly by white speakers.) But Joan does not use any of these stereotypically 'black' lexical items: rather, her Creole seems to be used in response to Carol's use of Creole. There is no evidence to suggest that Joan is trying to establish a 'black identity' as such.

Turning now to Carol's talk, we can see that not all of her speech is 'pure Creole'. Several of her sentences, and one com-plete turn (ll. 40–41) are LE. What are we to make of this? The explanation cannot be in terms of Carol's lack of *competence* in Creole, since she displays a knowledge of Creole forms throughout the conversation. Rather, we need to see Carol's use of both LE and Creole as part of a deliberate (though not necess-arily conscious) strategy of code switching for conversational ends. I will deal in detail with code switching in a later chapter. For the time being, notice that on two occasions, Carol interrupts the flow of her own talk, trying to remember when a particular event took place – and on both occasions her self-interruption is in LE, interrupting a Creole sequence:

15 C   <u>man (1.0) Leonie have party</u> (0.4) when? (1.2)
→   don' remember when it was <u>but she did tell all o' dem</u>
        <u>no fi- t say not'in'</u> (0.6)

27   <u>so me no care (2.0) don' really business</u>
→   (but) yeah, cause it was on the fifteenth innit (0.4)
        that time I was goin' out (to the) Bouncing Ball so (.)
30   even if she did invite me <u>me wouldn't a go</u>

Thus Carol's talk in this conversation can be analysed as mak-ing use of two distinct codes, 'Creole' and 'English', between which she moves systematically from time to time.

As a final illustration of the complexities of shifting between codes, take the following extract from a conversation between two boys, Chris and Samuel, both aged about fifteen:

Extract 4: Who's the girl?

1	C	free months ago
	S	's a <u>long</u> [laŋ] [P1] time
	C	I know i%s a <u>long</u> time but still
	S	Who's 'e gyal?
5	C	Don' know 'oo the girl is. You know 'er, don' know 'oo
	S	Who is di gyal, who di gyal
	C	Don' know who the gel is
	S	Who the gyal 'oo the gal 'oo the gal
	C	Nah she's she one in this school bu% I ain'% tellin' you

Samuel's repeated question *who is the girl?* takes several different forms. Each of the component words, *who, is, the* and *girl* has variant forms which can be associated with 'Creole' or 'LE', as follows:

word	'Creole'	'LE'
who	who [huː]	who [hʊː], 'oo [ʊ]
is	is, ø	is, 's
the	de [di]	[ðə ə və] (and others)
girl	gyal [gjæl]	girl [gɜː ɫ] [gɛɫ gɛo]
	gal [gæl]	

The first version, in line 4, of *who is the girl?* is probably Samuel's most 'London' version, although even here *girl* is *gyal* rather than the London *gel* which Chris uses consistently. The *next* version, in line 6, is the most unequivocally Creole, though typical of a 'mesolectal' style because of the presence of *is*, which would be *a* or omitted altogether in the basilect. (See pp. 28–30 for a discussion of these terms.) In fact Samuel omits *is* from this point on, and in this respect his repetitions of the phrase become more Creole; however, the consonant of *the* now starts to appear as [ð] (l. 8, three times), the pronunciation associated with 'Standard' both in Jamaica and Britain. The dropping of /h/ from *who*, also in l.8, could be a London or Jamaican phenomenon, but since initial /h/ is likely to occur in Jamaican under conditions of emphasis, this h-dropping looks more like London speech.

Samuel is one of the few informants in this study who was actually born in Jamaica and spent several years there. So the alternation in lines 6 and 8 between *is* and ø, [huː] and [ʊː] and [ðɪ] and [dɪ] may reflect stylistic alternations *within* the Jamaican continuum, roughly between 'basilect' and 'mesolect'. Even so, there are no neat correspondences: the Standard [ð] still sits with the non-standard [ʊ:] (whether [ʊ:] is Creole or London). While there seems to be one major code switch, from LE to Creole after line 4, there are several apparently inconsistent style shifts in lines 4 and 6.

Questions and approaches

The four extracts above raise some interesting and difficult questions about the language behaviour of their speakers.

It seems that young black Londoners who 'chat Patois' speak, on the one hand, a variety of language – 'Ordinary English' – which is very close to the norms of the LE of white speakers, and on the other, the language which Rosen and Burgess (1980) called 'London/Jamaican'. Up till now I have simply equated this with Jamaican Creole, and have based my comparisons on descriptions of that language by B.L. Bailey, J.C. Wells and others. But the question posed in Chapter 1 remains unanswered: is this language *really* JC, and if so, is the London variety any different from that spoken in Jamaica? And is there a range of speech styles/dialects involved, as in the Caribbean language situation, or is there just one variety?

Furthermore, what is the nature of the *London* English which black Londoners use? Should it be seen as a distinct variety in its own right, or is it no different from the 'ordinary' language of long-established communities of white Londoners?

Finally, is the language behaviour of these 'London Jamaican' speakers the sort of behaviour that characterises bilinguals, or is it more like the behaviour of monolinguals who style-shift from time to time in response to conversational and situational factors?

I shall try to answer these questions in the rest of this book. The approach I adopt here is based on the following principles:

(1) My study of individuals' linguistic behaviour is based on the close analysis of interactions within conversation. I have not attempted to use quantitative techniques or (with one exception) statistical analyses, believing that the close inspection of conversational data can tell us more about what 'London Jamaican' really is than any quantitative approach.

(2) First-language or native-speaker competence in LE is nearly universal among second-generation Caribbeans in London. For most speakers of 'Creole', Creole is actually a *second* language or variety. I shall argue in Chapter 4 that most of the adolescent Creole users are best treated as second *dialect* speakers of Creole rather than second *language* learners.

(3) All speakers recognise at least two distinct codes, 'Creole/Patois' or 'Black Talk' and London English (usually called just 'ordinary English'). Speakers are able to code switch between these in ways which their peer groups license as appropriate. Chapter 5 focuses on the London English variety of my Caribbean informants. Chapters 6 and 7 provide a detailed analysis of code switching behaviour.

Before going on to look at London Jamaican and Black London English in Chapters 4 and 5, I shall discuss some relevant research and theory relating to Caribbean Creoles in Chapter 3.

3 Continuum and Variation: Approaches to Describing Creole

Although a good deal has by now been written about the language and putative language problems of Caribbean children in British schools, remarkably little research has actually been done to study the linguistic behaviour of Caribbeans in Britain. In part this reflects research priorities set by policy makers at national level; in part it reflects the relatively weak position of the minority communities themselves; and of course these two causes are interrelated. Ideally, research within minority communities should be conducted by members of those communities, with the same facilities, resources and skills at their disposal as other researchers have. In practice, this is unlikely to happen except on a small scale in the present political climate.

Since J. C. Wells's research on the phonological adaptations made by Jamaicans who had lived for a period in London (Wells 1973), there have been only a few detailed studies of the language of Caribbeans in Britain in spite of a good deal of interest in all aspects of Britain's black population. Two of the best-known studies are Sutcliffe's Bedford Survey and subsequent work mainly in Bedford, reported in Sutcliffe (1982a), and the study of the black community in Dudley, West Midlands, carried out by Edwards, Sutcliffe and associates and reported in Edwards (1986). Apart from these, and the research described in the present book, there has been relatively little research in this area, most of it resulting in unpublished MA theses (e.g. Tate 1984) or doctoral theses (e.g. Wright 1984). This chapter will concentrate on questions of methodology: what approach is most suitable to the study of Creole use in the British context? Since much of the research done in Britain has been influenced in one way or another by linguistic research in the Caribbean, it will be necessary to refer to some of the theoretical approaches to the language situation there.

Diglossia and the 'post-Creole continuum'

In a situation where two *dissimilar* languages with unequal status – for example, Standard English and French Creole – coexist in one community, the dynamic which evolves between them may in theory lead to any one of several different states. For example, they may coexist in a 'stable diglossia' (Ferguson 1959) – with a strict differentiation of function between the 'high' and 'low' languages, or one may decline steadily at the expense of the other. Whichever of the possibilities is realised in practice, we would expect the two languages – Creole and *unrelated* Standard – to retain their integrity as languages and not to converge linguistically to any great extent, except in terms of vocabulary: in other words, they are likely to remain fundamentally dissimilar in their grammar and phonology. [1]

An illustration of this is to be found in Surinam on the Caribbean coast of South America. The vernacular of the coastal region, Sranan Tongo, is a Creole with English-based lexicon, already mentioned in Chapter 1. Following the displacement by the Dutch of the original English settlers, the Dutch language became the official and 'high' variety in Surinam and retains that status to this day. Standard English no longer had any status in the community and native speakers of English were almost entirely absent. As a result, Sranan bears little resemblance to English: its grammar and phonology have more in common with the African languages of the original slave population than with English, and its vocabulary, though largely English in origin, has undergone alterations which make it sound very unlike English: *Sranan kondre na wan asi-tere; wan dey a way so, a trawan a way so.* 'Surinam (country) is a horse's tail: one day it waves so (this way), another day it waves so (that way).'

By contrast, in many ex-British territories of the Caribbean, Standard English coexists with an English-based Creole. This is true, for example, in Jamaica, Guyana, Trinidad, Belize, Grenada, and Montserrat, as well as in other territories. It is also true of

Barbados, though this has been questioned: Barbadian ('Bajan') is somewhat less different from British English than Jamaican, Guyanese, etc. In these places today, Standard English exists as a model which members of the community may aspire to, though not all choose to do so. Certainly the education system encourages them to, by valuing only the Standard in most territories. Creole does not have high status in the 'mainstream' culture anywhere in the ex-British Caribbean.

The notion of a 'post-Creole continuum', first put forward by De Camp (1971), is an attempt to explain the complex linguistic situation in those places where there is a long history of native speakers of British English in contact with speakers of an English-based Creole. It applies to the case where two highly-focused varieties of language (see Le Page and Tabouret-Keller, 1985: 115), with identifiably similar vocabulary but social statuses at polar extremes, coexist in one society. The 'continuum' which is said to link the high and low varieties results from the fact that individuals in the community have differential access to these varieties depending on their social status and social relationships at home and at work. If individuals in the society (except for those at the very top and the very bottom of the social ladder) are socially mobile in each direction to some extent, then the 'continuum' can be seen as consisting of a collection of individuals whose linguistic competences in intermediate varieties (or 'lects') overlap to form an unbroken chain linking the archetypal Creole (or 'basilect') with the Standard (or 'acrolect'). Here is De Camp's description of the continuum as it applies to Jamaica (1971:350):

> no one can deny the extreme variability of Jamaican English . . . in Jamaica there is no sharp cleavage between Creole and standard. Rather there is a linguistic continuum, a continuous spectrum of speech varieties ranging from the 'bush talk' or 'broken language' of Quashie [sic] to the educated standard of Philip Sherlock and Norman Manley. Many Jamaicans persist in the myth that there are only two varieties: the patois and the standard. But one speaker's attempt at the patois may be closer to the standard end of the spectrum than is another speaker's attempt at the standard. The 'standard' is not standard British, as many Jamaicans claim: rather it is an evolving standard Jamaican (or perhaps standard West Indian) English which is mutually intelligible with, but undeniably different from, standard British. *Each Jamaican speaker*

commands a span of this continuum, the breadth of the span de-
pending on the breadth of his [sic] social contacts (emphasis mine
– MS)

Linguists such as C.-J. N. Bailey (e.g. 1973) and Bickerton (e.g.
1973, 1975) have claimed that the continuum of 'lects' between
'basilect' and 'acrolect' can be characterised by a series of rules
which convert each lect, starting from basilect, into the next up-
ward lect. Bickerton (1973) provides detailed analyses using statistical scaling of variables to produce an implicational scale,
ranking different speakers' grammars in such a way that each
grammar (corresponding to a 'lect') differs from the next by just
one rule. Crucial to the arguments of Bailey and Bickerton is the
scaleability of their data, which is intended to show that the rules
are added in a set order (reflecting the historical development –
the 'decreolisation' of the language), and resulting in a systematic
ordering of lects from bottom to top. Thus speakers do not ran-
domly mix acrolect features with those from the basilect to create
a 'mesolect'; each 'lect' is discrete and ordered with respect to the
other lects in the continuum.

There appears to be prima facie a good case for the existence
of a dialect continuum in the Caribbean, given the social forces
and conditions that have shaped life and language there in the
last three centuries. Alleyne (1980: 184) attributes the post-Creole
continuum to the social stratification of the old plantation society
itself:

> whereas there was a high degree of sociological homogeneity with-
> in the slave population arising from the fact that it was a slave
> population, this society was hierarchically structured in terms of
> status of occupation, privileges, and access to the culture of the
> masters. This produced a certain cultural and behavioural differen-
> tiation in the slave population, among whom language differences
> must have been highly significant.

In the more liberal social conditions of the post- emancipation
era, the local standard has become more accessible to most of the
population, thus strengthening the 'continuum' and allowing
more speakers to enter its middle and upper ranges. As a result,
the speakers of both 'broadest' Creole (basilect) and 'standard'
(acrolect) are a relatively small minority, with most of the popula-

tion speaking something located in between – or rather, commanding a continuous 'range of lects' somewhere between the basilect and acrolect.

To substantiate the continuum hypothesis De Camp and others (for example, Bickerton, in his detailed studies of Guyanese Creole) point to the following well-documented facts: few Jamaicans or Guyanese speak Standard English, few speak maximally broad Creole all the time: most speak (by their own assessment as well as a linguist's) something 'in between'; and how close to the standard or the broad Creole they speak, is largely a function of their social class. For Bickerton, the continuum – a dynamic system of lects – is necessary to explain the complexities of the Guyanese linguistic situation: 'for Guyanese Creole clearly does not constitute a language, in so far as one end of it is indistinguishable from English' (Bickerton 1973: 166).

However, the notion of a 'post-Creole continuum' is not accepted by all linguists. Romaine (1982: 177–82) discusses Bickerton's data at some length, reevaluating his criteria for scaling variables. Romaine does not deny that implicational relationships exist in language, but concludes (citing De Camp 1971 as an example) that 'the problem is that some linguists seem to be quite willing to put forward very arbitrary implicational scales without justifying them.' (1982: 182)

Studies by Le Page and Tabouret-Keller have provided a further critique on the continuum hypothesis, again denying the scalability of phonological and grammatical variables which is said to lead speakers on a unidirectional, one-step-at-a-time path from the basilect to the acrolect. This neat orderliness has been attacked by Le Page and Tabouret-Keller, who write (1985: 198):

> Such a model necessarily implies a linear sequence of varieties within 'a language', with the implication that all innovation starts from the same source and travels in the same direction; and that innovation in phonology is paralleled by a similar sequence of innovation in different parts of the grammar and lexicon. None of these suppositions can be sustained

Notwithstanding its critics, the continuum hypothesis has been an influential one in the study of Caribbean Creoles, and has formed the basis for significant studies of at least two of the Caribbean territories, Jamaica (De Camp 1971) and Guyana

(Bickerton 1973, 1975) Whatever the merits of the continuum hypothesis as a linguistic *theory*, its terms, 'acrolect' for the local standard, 'basilect' for the broad Creole, 'mesolect' for the in-between varieties used mainly by the middle classes, have become widely accepted. What is more, it has been taken up for use in other situations, so that J.C. Wells, for example, applies it to socially stratified varieties of British English (Wells 1982: 18). While the terms 'acrolect', 'mesolect', 'basilect' are, as Wells writes, 'a convenient terminology', it needs to be borne in mind that substantial, and by no means universally accepted, theoretical claims underlie the continuum hypothesis itself.

A British continuum?

Any claim for the existence of a 'post-Creole continuum' among second generation speakers in Britain is shaky from the start. Romaine, Le Page and Tabouret-Keller and others have raised serious theoretical objections to the continuum hypothesis itself, as described above. However, since the notion of a continuum persists in the literature it warrants some further discussion.

Sutcliffe (1982a) argued that in Britain, 'JC is a language caught up with English in a dialect continuum . . . nearly all Jamaican language in Jamaica, as well as in Britain, is neither (extreme) Creole nor English but falls in between, "on the continuum." ' (p. 115). However, 'it is almost certainly true that JC is a separate or at least separable language from English, as an abstract system, as a psychological reality to its speakers, and even as an actual spoken variety.'

Sutcliffe himself is aware of the difficulty of reconciling these two statements. More recently, he has emphasised the second view, stating (1982b) 'rather than "decreolisation", we have: variation *within* Creole; variation *within* English, as well as switching between the two . . . The middle of the "continuum" tends to be unimportant or nonexistent, in this country at least. So speakers are left with, basically, two main speech varieties' (p. 115).

This view is supported by Sutcliffe's own data, as well as mine, which shows Black British speakers focusing on the JC basilect when 'chattin' Patois', even though they do not always hit their target as intended.

Wright (1984) makes a similar point in discussing the narrative style of one of Sutcliffe's speakers, Malcolm, which she contrasts with one of her own informants, Tania. Malcolm, a sixteen year-old boy living in Luton, apparently controlled several different registers between Creole and Standard. On hearing a recording of a sentence that was 'JC but not quite the JC extreme' (Sutcliffe 1982a: 124) he offered to tell a story in a language that was 'more Jamaican' than what he had just heard. The story he then told is described by Sutcliffe as 'paradigmatic Baileyan JC'.

Tania, Wright's informant, was a ten year-old girl from Kingston, Jamaica. Wright comments: 'Comparison of the two passages shows clearly that while Malcolm focuses on the basilect, Tania's narrative is more diffuse. It uses a wide range of lects, for dramatic effect.' Wright showed Malcolm's and Tania's narratives to Jamaican-born informants: their consensus was that Tania's narrative was 'typical of the [Jamaican] speech community' in using a range of lects. Malcolm's story was unusual from a Jamaican perspective in that 'it lacks the usual mixing of JC and JSE forms as in Tania's narrative . . . Many of my informants felt that the use of "JC" features is stereotyped and that these British adolescents do not speak "real Jamaican." ' (Wright 1984: 41).

Again, we find that Wright's British data suggests a *mixing of separate* varieties rather than a post-Creole continuum.

The Caribbean continuum, as it has been theorised by De Camp, Alleyne and others, is dependent on the existence of social stratification which is directly reflected through language. But the class and regional differences – linguistic and cultural – of the Caribbean have been maintained in Britain for at most one generation in their original form. The second and third generations (the generations of my informants) have not simply reproduced the class stratification of the Caribbean region, nor have they merged seamlessly into the already existing class strata of British society. Rather, in Gilroy's words:

> New types of class relations are being shaped and reproduced in the novel economic conditions which we inhabit. The scale of these changes, which can be glimpsed through the pertinence of a populist politics of 'race' and nation, is such that it calls the vocabulary and analytic frameworks of class analysis into question. It emphasises the fact that class is not something given in economic antagonisms which can be expressed straightforwardly in political formations. (Gilroy 1987: 34)

There is thus no reason for the social class 'lects' of the Caribbean to exist among black youth in Britain. A linguistic 'continuum' must *ex hypothesi* reflect a social continuum of speakers who have differential access to the 'top' and 'bottom' varieties. We shall see that in fact, Black British speakers focus on the *broadest* Creole variety, though they *code switch* between this and British English to an extent which varies from individual to individual and from situation to situation. While in Caribbean society, use of the basilect is associated with low social status (and possibly rural origins), in Britain it is a sign of ethnic identity and solidarity, providing an in-group language for adolescents. Sutcliffe makes a similar observation: 'the real motivation for selecting one dialect or another has relatively little to do with the English class system as such and a great deal to do with ethnic and cultural identification.' (1982: 14).

Code switching between varieties

Another way of looking at the variation found in the Caribbean is in terms of *code switching*. Code switching is a common type of behaviour among bilinguals in many communities where the use of two or more languages is widespread and stable. It assumes the existence of at least two distinct languages or language varieties. The bilingual individual 'mixes' these languages or varieties ('codes') by alternating ('switching') between them – sometimes at the boundary between two sentences, but often within a sentence. Poplack (1980) demonstrated that this type of behaviour is characteristic of *fluent* bilinguals, and is not motivated just by 'incomplete knowledge' of one of the languages.

A great deal has been written about code switching, from various viewpoints: social, pragmatic, grammatical. However, little of this literature bears *directly* on the case of Creole. It is widely accepted among researchers that for code switching to take place, speakers must recognise at least two distinct codes, i.e. two distinct language systems. This immediately creates some problems, since 'codes' for this purpose are social constructs, and do not necessarily coincide with what *linguists* would recognise as discrete languages. What to linguists using purely linguistic criteria might be two different languages, or two closely related dialects, may *to their speakers* be two dialects of the same language, or two different languages respectively. Gumperz discusses this in the following terms:

> the bilingual phenomena we are concerned with are usually accompanied by extensive convergence and structural overlap . . . sentences in language pairs which seem quite distinct from the monolingual perspective may appear to be almost identical on the surface . . . To juxtapose such sequences in natural conversational contexts, participants must be sensitive to what to the outsider may appear as quite subtle perceptual cues (Gumperz (1982: 85).

It is differences of this order that separate 'Creole' from 'English' and which complicate an analysis of Caribbean speakers' linguistic behaviour in terms of code-switching. However, much of the research on code-switching to date (Gumperz's own work being the main exception) has dealt with much more readily separable codes such as Spanish/English (e.g. Poplack 1980) or Italian/German (e.g. Auer 1984a).

Lawton (1980) is critical of the 'continuum hypothesis' as it applies to Jamaica. He puts forward as an alternative a model of a two-language system with code switching between systems, citing B. L. Bailey's (1966) description of the grammar of 'Jamaican Creole' as an indication that 'Creole' (the basilect) can be described as a discrete system. He reports experimental evidence which suggests that adolescent middle-class Jamaicans can distinguish 'Jamaican English' from 'Jamaican Creole', and shows that code switching between these two can be identified not only in contemporary speech, but also in the speech of characters in literary texts. In fact the existence of code-switching is not incompatible with the continuum hypothesis, since speakers could presumably switch between different lects at the extremes of their own range.

In the case of the language of young black Creole users in Britain, an analysis of at least *some* of their behaviour in terms of code switching seems to be accepted by all researchers. (See, for example, the views of Sutcliffe and Edwards in the next section.) It will form a key element of the analysis of the data presented in this book.

Edwards and Sutcliffe: a variationist approach

Edwards (1986), based on research carried out by Viv Edwards, David Sutcliffe, and their fieldworkers Carol Tomlin and Leighton Bruce, is a study within the 'variationist' tradition. The researchers made recordings of black adolescents in five different situations, in an attempt to control the variables of race of inter-locutor, gender and formality/informality. The situations were: 'White formal interview' (i.e. a formal interview situation where the interviewer was white); 'Black formal interview' (a formal in-terview situation where the interviewer was black); 'racially mixed informal conversation', 'Black peer group conversation', 'Black informal conversation with fieldworker'. For the second and fifth of these situations, the subjects were segregated by gen-der, the male group being left with a male fieldworker, and the female with a female fieldworker. In a controversial aspect of the data collection, the subjects were allowed to think that the tape recorder had been switched off after the formal interviews, and were encouraged to talk informally by a young white member of the research team, who dissociated himself from the preceding interviews and 'spent the duration of the recording sitting on the floor' (Edwards 1986: 74). In addition to the recording of all the talk, formal and informal, a questionnaire was used to collect information on community involvement, education, lifestyles (church-goer, Rastafarian, etc.), and 'acquiescence' or 'criticalness' of attitude toward mainstream white society. Other questions were designed to elicit information about extent of Creole use as perceived by the respondent.

Edwards and Sutcliffe used the recorded data to make a 'Patois index' for each speaker in each of the five situations. Eleven fea-tures characteristic of Creole were used, and the formula

$$\frac{\text{No. of tokens of Patois variant}}{\text{No. of tokens of Patois and English variants}} \times 100$$

was applied to find a frequency score for each variable. The index was constructed using the mean scores for the 11 variables (Edwards 1986: 79). This index showed that the most Patois usage was in situation 4, where the subjects were left alone with-out a fieldworker present, or situation 5, chatting informally with the black fieldworker ('Black informal conversation with field-worker'). In situations 1–3 there was not much difference between the Patois scores, but it was significantly lower than in the other two situations. The researchers found that criticalness/acquiescence, sex and education (in interaction with each other) and social network had significant effects on the Patois index (pp. 82–6).

Edwards and Sutcliffe's use of the 'Patois index' can be criticised on the grounds that it does not take into account code-switching behaviour. Edwards acknowledges the importance of code switching in the community under study:

> Close examination of British Black speech suggests that the situation is closer to that of a bilingual community than to the post-Creole continuum which operates in the Caribbean. Code-switching behaviour, which has been reported as a regular feature of stable bilingual communities . . . is certainly a common feature of much in-group speech (p. 49).

She also acknowledges the effect of code-switching on the Patois index: 'In practice, because Patois was usually used in conjunction with English as a part of code-switching behaviour, most scores were considerably nearer to 100 than they were to 0' (p.79). However, these scores hide as much as they reveal. If code switching is a regular feature of *all* speech styles in British black English, except perhaps the most formal, then the index of each speaker will actually be based on two distinct, discontinuous stretches of speech; one which will have a Patois index of 100 or very close, (i.e. *no* Patois features, because it is actually not meant to be Patois, but 'English') and another – the Patois part – which will have a Patois index closer to 0. What the index will then be measuring is the *proportion* in which the speakers mix Patois and English. Since some speakers (those who have low 'competence') do not use many Patois features anyway, these speakers will have a lower Patois index than other speakers who code switch to the same extent, but who use more Patois features in the Patois part of their talk. The Patois index therefore tells us everything and nothing about an individual speaker: it tells us whether that person uses many or few Patois features overall in their talk, but nothing about how he or she *uses* Patois and English as part of a communicative strategy.

Creole acquisition as second language learning?

Edwards and Sutcliffe also constructed a 'Patois Competence Scale'. ('Competence' here refers to language abilities, not the Chomskyan notion of innate tacit knowledge of a language.) They identified twenty features of grammar or phonology which characterise 'Patois' as opposed to British English. Speakers were given a score of one point for each one of these features that occurred in their speech, irrespective of how many times it occurred. The researchers found a wide variation in 'Patois competence', with scores ranging from 8 to 20 (p. 96). They found that about one-third of their sample were 'very fluent speakers who confidently use the full range of Patois features'. However, about a quarter 'can only be described as having limited competence in Patois' (p. 100). Edwards describes the behaviour of this group as 'highly reminiscent of that of second language learners', using the data from the Patois competence scores and statistical methods drawn from second language acquisition research, to arrive at an 'acquisitional hierarchy' for British black speakers. She says, 'it is clear that the various features of Patois are learned neither at random nor in isolation. Rather, groups of structures appear to be acquired in set orders across a population of speakers' (p. 103). The result is that the twenty features of the Patois competence scale can be grouped into five clusters. Each cluster of features is acquired at about the same time, but not all speakers – now seen as 'learners' – go through all five stages. Some never go beyond the first.

The leap from competence scores (which do not *really* measure competence, but only use) to 'acquisitional hierarchy' – in the meantime having identified speakers of Patois as second language learners – seems unjustified. The conclusion that some speakers use more, and some fewer, Creole features, is undoubtedly correct and is borne out by my London data. But the existence of an implicational hierarchy alone cannot justify treating speakers as second language learners, in the absence of evidence that acquisition is actually going on. Edwards does relate the socialisation patterns of speakers to their Patois competence: 'The degree of speakers' integration into the black community as measured by their network score would thus appear to be the most important determinant of their Patois competence. The opportunity to be with other Patois speakers and to both hear and use Patois is obviously critical' (p.105). This is consistent with the hypothesis that Patois features are acquired through socialisation – however, it does not demonstrate that that is what is really happening.

Before taking the idea that British black English users are second language learners of Patois any further, we need to look at the social and linguistic conditions in which Patois exists among second-generation Caribbeans in Britain. To decide whether they really are learning Creole as a second *language*, we need information about at least two areas: (1) the age of acquisition; (2) the nature of the process of acquisition itself. Unfortunately, in the second of these areas, we have a complete blank. We truly know *nothing* of the socialisation processes by which young black people in Britain acquire Creole. In Hewitt (1986) we have an account in some detail of the processes by which white children acquire Creole by socialisation with black peers, but so far there have been no studies which have focused on how the black children acquire Creole in the first place. Edwards and Sutcliffe's study was based on a single session with each individual. Though their data may suggest an 'acquisitional hierarchy' the actual *process* is not visible in their research. As regards the age of acquisition, there are conflicting reports.

An adolescent phenomenon?

The age at which an individual learns a language has profound implications for proficiency in that language. 'In general, Lenneberg's (1967) contention that the extent to which a speaker will have a foreign accent correlates fairly well with the age at which the second language is learned has received extensive confirmation. There are some studies which support the claim that early acquisition also seems to make for better syntactic ability' (Romaine 1989: 214–15). Most researchers have focused on Creole use in Britain as an adolescent phenomenon, and there seems to be a general belief that use of Creole is negligible or non-existent before the age of 14 or so. Edwards writes: 'Various writers, (e.g. Crump 1979) refer to teacher reports that the speech of young black children closely resembles that of their white peers until about the ages of 14 or 15'. Rosen and Burgess (1980) report a low rate of Patois usage among twelve year-old children in London. Edwards sees this as 'probably not insignificant' (1986: 55) as the children in that survey fell below the 'critical age' of fourteen or fifteen. Hewitt (1986) observes that 'black youngsters themselves often reach a peak of Creole use in their late teens' (p. 193) while where white Creole users are concerned, 'most youngsters who employ Creole cease to do so at about the age of sixteen'.

On the other hand, Creole use *begins* much earlier for some children; Hewitt observes that there is *less* use of Creole in primary schools than in secondary schools, but that it is not absent altogether. In 'Area B', one of two areas of South-East London where Hewitt worked and one which has a relatively high density of Caribbeans, even white children may learn some Creole in primary school, through peer contact (1986: 150). In Birmingham, use of Creole by primary school children has been reported and tape recordings have been made (G. Power, personal communication). And in the London Jamaican study, I found many black twelve and thirteen year-olds with a knowledge of Creole, some of whom were very avid users of it. It appears that the notion that use of Patois or Creole is an *exclusively* adolescent phenomenon is an oversimplification. It may be that Creole is just more *visible*, more *public* in the years fourteen to seventeen, say.

Creole – 'second language' or 'new dialect'?

Black children acquiring Creole may be going through a process not of *second language acquisition* but of *new dialect acquisition*. There is a small literature on new dialect acquisition; it must be said that not a great deal is known about it. In some ways it is similar to second language acquisition, but it appears to be different in that it starts from the natively acquired dialect as a base.

When a speaker S who speaks a particular variety V1 of a language L moves to an area where the local language is, in terms of speakers' own assessments, a different variety of the same language L – in other words, a different dialect of L – say, V2, it is usual for that individual's speech to acquire some of the phonological and grammatical characteristics of V2. Since perfect learning of a new language *or* dialect is very rare beyond the age of, say, fourteen, (see the discussion in the last section; also Trudgill 1986: 34; Romaine 1984: 190ff), the usual result is that S's personal variety shows some features of V1 (the variety of S's 'native' community) and some features of V2. Thus what S speaks – though it clearly is a variety of L – is not quite V1 and not quite V2, but a third variety, V3. Such a personal dialect or variety is usually termed an *idiolect*.

The acquisition of Creole by London-born Caribbeans is similar to acquiring a new dialect, in the sense that British English and Jamaican Creole share much of their grammar, phonology and lexis. It is different in that rather than *lose* V1 altogether in favour of V2, the London speakers of Creole use V2 *alongside* V1. In this respect the situation is closer to the acquisition of a second language, with resultant bilingualism.

In the next chapter I shall discuss the Creole of young black Londoners in more detail, and argue the case for treating them as 'new dialect learners' rather than 'second language learners'.

Note

1. This is not to rule out the possibility of language convergence in terms of grammar, lexis and phonology, which has been reported in a number of cases. See Romaine 1989: 66–9 for a discussion of these possible 'long-term effects of language contact and bilingualism'.

4 *London* Jamaican...?

In earlier centuries, the inhabitants of the British Isles had a tradition of settling in other parts of the world, establishing English-speaking communities in, for example, North America, Australia, South Africa and New Zealand. Each of these has its own local variety of English, which is different from any indigenous British variety. In these former colonies, *new* dialects of English arose out of contact between speakers of different dialects native to the British Isles.

The situation in the Caribbean was significantly different in that the process of 'dialect creation' actually involved the creation of new *languages* through the processes of *pidginisation* and *creolisation*, and subsequently, *decreolisation* – as the Creole grew closer to Standard through prolonged contact with the lexifier language (the language which contributed most of the vocabulary – in this case, English).

However, once these new languages and varieties had become established in the Caribbean, the same phenomenon of migration took their speakers back to the original 'homeland' of the lexifier language, English. Has this led to the existence of 'overseas dialects' of the Caribbean Creoles, in the same way that migration has led to the American, Canadian, Australian and other overseas dialects of English?

'Focusing' and 'Diffusion'

One way of understanding the processes which are involved in the formation of new dialects is in terms of Le Page's concepts *focusing* and *diffusion* (Le Page and Tabouret-Keller 1985). These are social processes which are present, to some extent, in every language situation. *Focusing* involves a speech community in establishing and adhering to rather narrow norms of linguistic behaviour, i.e. putting fairly strict limits on the range of acceptable forms. Sometimes these forms are overtly referred to and talked about, for example in those communities which have clear notions of 'correct' grammar and 'standard' language. In such communities the focused norms may be codified in dictionaries and grammars, and there may be penalties (such as educational failure) for individuals who do not adhere to the norm.

On the other hand, other linguistic communities may have more relaxed norms. Such communities may tolerate a wide range of different forms to express the same item. Diversity may not be treated as remarkable, and 'deviance' will be defined differently as a wider range of possibilities will be treated as normal. Such a community has, in Le Page's terms, 'diffuse' norms.

'Focusing' and 'diffusion' are processes inherent in many linguistic situations: focusing, for example, is a necessary part of standardisation, while diffusion may characterise situations where speakers of different languages or language varieties come into contact. Le Page and Tabouret-Keller write:

> As the individual speaks he [*sic*] is seen as always using language with reference to the inner models of the universe he has constructed for himself; he projects in words images of that universe (or, of those universes) on to the social screen, and these images may be more or less sharply focussed, or more or less diffuse, in relation to each other or in relation to those projected by others in their interaction with him . . . Language . . . is the instrument through which, by means of individual adjustments in response to feedback, both 'languages' and 'groups' may become more highly focused in the sense that the behaviour of members of a group may become more alike . . . 'Focusing' will imply greater regularity in the linguistic code, less variability; 'diffusion' the converse.
> (Le Page and Tabouret-Keller (1985: 115–16))

The creation of a new, relatively stable language variety from different sources – as in a new dialect emerging from a number of different dialects spoken by settlers who speak different dialects of the same language – can be viewed as a focusing process.

Trudgill writes:

> The reduction of variants that accompanies focusing, in the course
> of *new-dialect formation*, takes place via the process of *koinéiza-*
> *tion*. This comprises the process of *levelling*, which involves the
> loss of marked and/or minority variants; and the process of *simpli-*
> *fication*, by means of which even minority forms may be the ones
> to survive if they are linguistically simpler, in the technical sense,
> and through which even forms and distinctions present in all the
> contributory dialects may be lost. (Trudgill 1986: 126)

Given what we know about the formation of new varieties of
English in overseas colonies of Britain, we might expect a similar
process to have taken place among Caribbean migrants living in
Britain itself. As the Caribbean Creoles are all fairly similar to
each other, we might have expected Trudgill's processes of 'levelling' and 'simplification' to have applied to produce a 'British Caribbean Creole' sharing features of all the Caribbean Creoles with
significant numbers of speakers in Britain. This would apply, of
course, to the second and subsequent Creole-speaking generations
in Britain. The first generation might practise some 'levelling' –
an adaptation and 'evening-out' of any highly marked regional-
isms in their speech – but would basically stick to the linguistic
habits they brought with them from the Caribbean.

However, this is *not* what has happened. Young black Londoners do *not* speak a 'British Caribbean Creole' with features
drawn from many Caribbean varieties. Rather, they acknowledge
two distinct and separable codes. When they are not speaking
London English, they may choose to 'talk black' or 'chat Patois':
but this 'black' variety, as I shall show below, is focused on
Jamaican Creole in particular. This focusing on JC has been
noted by many writers, and is the basis for the term 'London
Jamaican' which has been current at least since Rosen and Burgess (1980).

The situation seems to be similar in other parts of the country.
For example, Wright, describing the language behaviour of young
black residents of Birmingham, talks of 'recreolisation', whereby
speakers focus on a norm maximally distinct (or nearly so) from
the Standard. (Note that 'recreolisation' can also mean the development of a *new* Creole language from an existing one which has

undergone pidginisation for a second time. This is not the sense in which it is used here.) Wright remarks that Sutcliffe's data (1982a: 124) support the notion (attributed to Le Page) that 're-creolisation is a focusing process'. Sutcliffe's data

> show that these speakers have a very clear idea of what, for them, constitutes a basilectal utterance. In other words, they show evidence that the target language is 'an abstraction' of JC, a focusing on phonological and morphological patterns, lexicon and syntactic structures which are distinct from Standard English. (Wright (1984: 37)

Edwards, also describing a black community in the West Midlands, comments on 'the preference for basilectal rather than mesolectal forms' (Edwards 1986: 104).

Further evidence for 'recreolisation' involving focusing on the Jamaican basilect comes from research in Bradford by S. Tate already mentioned (Tate 1984; Sebba and Tate 1986). Bradford is unusual among British cities in that the largest group of Caribbeans in the city are not Jamaicans, but Dominicans. Dominica is one of the Eastern Caribbean islands where a French Creole is spoken by the older generation. While no systematic research has been done on language use within families in the Bradford Dominican community, Tate considers that her informants, who were Rastafarian members of a band, had competence in JC on a par with natives of Jamaica (Tate is herself Jamaican-born). Since the parents are presumed to be native speakers of Dominican French Creole, (they probably speak a variety of Caribbean English as well) the Bradford Dominican speakers of JC must have acquired it through peer contact in their own community – where Jamaicans are a minority.

Leaving aside this rather striking example of language shift, what can we say about the role of JC for young black Londoners? There are relatively few points of difference between JC and the other Caribbean English-based Creoles that might enable us to pinpoint their focus as JC rather than some other variety. However, those differences which *do* exist point to JC rather than any other Creole as the focus. For example, the vowel sounds of FACE and GOAT have differing pronunciations in different parts of the Caribbean, and in the basilect and acrolect:

Table 4.1 FACE and GOAT vowels of the Caribbean

Language	FACE	GOAT
Jamaican Creole	[iɛ]	[uɔ]
Jamaican Standard	[e:]	[o:]
Trinidadian	/e/	/o/
Guyanese	/e:/	/o:/
Barbadian	/e:/	/o:/
Montserrat (acrolect)	[e:]	[o:]
Montserrat (basilect)	[ie]	[uɔ]
St Kitts-Nevis (acrolect)	/e:/	/o:/
St Kitts-Nevis (basilect)	/ia/	/ua/

Sources: J.C. Wells (1982, ch. 7) except for St Kitts-Nevis: Trudgill, 1986: 88–9

We see that JC, together with the basilectal varieties of Montserrat and St Kitts-Nevis, is distinctive in having an opening diphthong as the vowel of FACE and GOAT. The other varieties, both Standard and basilectal, have close pure vowels which are long, except in the case of Trinidadian. If 'focusing' in this case were to involve *levelling* as part of new dialect creation, then we might expect /e:/ and /o:/ to become the new focus, as they are the majority variants, the prestige variants almost everywhere, and arguably simpler in phonological terms than the others. But this is not what has happened: at least, my data shows no sign of it. The 'Patois' vowel for GOAT is typically [uɔ] and for FACE, [iɛ], just as in JC: see, for example, the Patois 'performances' of Susan and Joan in Chapter 2, who both use the Jamaican form [P5,P6] (see Appendix 1 for an explanation of the grammatical and phonological features in square brackets). While Montserrat and St Kitts-Nevis could plausibly provide the focus on the basis of the phonological evidence, it is unlikely in practice, as there are so few speakers of those varieties in Britain. They are heavily outnumbered by Jamaicans as well as, probably, Trinidadians and Guyanese. The evidence suggests that in London, too, the focus of 'black talk' is JC.

Creole learning as new dialect acquisition

It is well established (see, for example, Giles and Smith 1979) that speakers accommodate to other speakers – in other words, make their speech more similar to that of their interlocutor(s) – for a variety of social reasons. Accommodation is a significant driving factor in the process of new dialect formation as described by Trudgill (1986), but it is more easily studied at the level of individuals who adjust their language behaviour given a particular set of circumstances. Speakers who move to a new dialect area may, over time, adjust their speech, or 'accommodate', in the direction of the new dialect – with varying degrees of success. For example, an English person who lives for some time in the United States will often acquire a 'partially' American accent. However, unless they move at a very early age, such people rarely sound 'totally' American. Trudgill begins by trying to identify those features which are accommodated to most readily or earlier than others. As a way of studying *accommodation* – which for the most part is unconscious – he looked at *imitation*, in particular, the imitation of American accents by British pop singers. His conclusion is that accommodation involves a similar process to imitation, and in both cases, the key factor is the *salience* of particular features. Salient features are those features of a dialect which are likely to be imitated by a would-be mimic, or accommodated to by a would-be member of the community. Salience, of course, means salience for the hearer, and is therefore a relative term: those features of New York English which are salient for a Londoner may not be those which are salient for someone from Toronto.

As a speaker's speech undergoes a process of accommodation to the norms of the new dialect, a new grammar is acquired through the addition to the speaker's internal grammar of rules which 'convert' the existing dialect forms into the new ones. In many cases, features of the new dialect are learned in a set order: this is called the 'fixed route' hypothesis by Trudgill (1986). The result is an implicational scale which looks like the 'acquisitional hierarchy' proposed by Edwards and Sutcliffe.

However, Trudgill also shows that different speakers may follow different routes towards complete acquisition of a new dialect. Drawing on research by Nordenstam (1979), Rogers (1981) and Trudgill (1982), Trudgill reaches the conclusion that the fixed route of acquisition is confined

> to adults, or perhaps more probably to adolescents. Clearly, accommodation by children may be a very different kind of phe-

nomenon from accommodation by adults . . . Just as young
children are not inhibited by, say, phonotactic constraints in learning a foreign language, so they are equally uninhibited in acquiring
a different dialect. They therefore have much more freedom and
scope for accommodation, and are much less likely to conform to
the same fixed pattern. (Trudgill, 1982, p. 31)

Once again, the question of *age* of acquisition is important in
determining the relevance of the process of new dialect acquisition to the learning of Creole. If 'Creole' is a second dialect
rather than a second language, delaying its acquisition until adolescence will still have a limiting effect on how well it can be
learned. It is interesting that Trudgill finds that new dialect acquisition is more likely to follow the 'fixed route' in *older* learners. This would be in accordance with the 'acquisition hierarchy'
observed by Edwards, assuming that the acquisition is of a second dialect rather than a new language altogether.

New dialect acquisition is a more attractive explanation of the
London Creole speakers' behaviour than second language acquisition for several reasons. First of all, from the point of view of the
linguist, the similarities between JC and British English are sufficient that one might – using the vagueness of the term 'dialect' to
maximum advantage – call the two languages 'related dialects'.
More importantly, this is the relationship as it is *perceived* by
many speakers, both in the Caribbean and in Britain. Whatever
the similarities from the point of view of the linguist, from the
point of view of the *learner* acquiring a new dialect must seem a
very different process from acquiring a new language. Whereas
the difficulties in learning a new language are largely in its differences from the speaker's first language, the pitfalls of acquiring
a new dialect lie mainly in its similarities with the speaker's existing dialect. Since the underlying systems are similar but not identical, the learner must formulate rules which will successfully
convert the underlying forms into the surface forms of the new
dialect. If s/he is unsuccessful, the consequences in terms of communication failure will only occasionally be severe. Most of the
time the learner will be understood, but identified as an out-
group member. The gains and losses for the new dialect learner
are therefore mostly social, and the incentives or disincentives to
acquire particular linguistic forms are directly related to the symbolic value of those forms within the community.

The idea that the features of a dialect which are accommodated to are those which are most salient, and that those which are most salient from the point of view of a LE speaker are just those which are most different from LE, fits perfectly with the observation that young black speakers in 'chattin' Patois' are focusing on the Jamaican basilect – the variety which is *most different* from Standard. Thus the very *distinctiveness* of the Creole becomes the point to focus on – and therein lies its symbolic value as a variety maximally opposed to Standard English.

Accommodation in dialect contact

We have already seen that the social activity of 'chattin' Patois' involves a speaker's using *relatively* more Creole features than s/he usually does when speaking 'ordinary English'. While basilectal JC, as an abstraction of all that is maximally different from Standard (in B.L. Bailey's terms) may be an absolute, the socially constructed 'Patois' of the young black Londoners is relative to a norm of English/Creole use. For many speakers, 'chattin' Patois' simply means adding certain Creole features of grammar, phonology and lexis to what is essentially their normal brand of London English. This is particularly so for white Creole speakers who *cannot*, except in very rare and exceptional circumstances, have had exposure to Creole as young children: but it is also true for speakers like Stephen and Joan, whose 'Patois' approaches, but only sometimes reaches, the Jamaican Creole target.

In the rest of this chapter I will discuss Creole acquisition in terms of new dialect acquisition, with JC assumed to be the target variety.

Salience

According to Trudgill (1986: 37) it is 'salient features of the target variety that are adjusted to, except that, in the case of adults at least, a number of factors combine to delay this modification to different extents'. But what exactly makes a feature salient? Trudgill identifies a number of factors relating to accent (i.e. phonology only), of which two are most important: *degree of phonetic difference* and, more importantly, *surface phonemic contrast* (Trudgill 1986: 37). This means that the most significant features of accent which are imitated/accommodated to will be (1) features involving a phonemic contrast, in other words, points where the sound *systems* of two varieties, rather than just the sounds themselves, are different; (2) points of pronunciation where the systems themselves are not different, but the sounds representing a particular phoneme are substantially different.

As an example of (1) – a difference in phonological systems – we could take the difference between rhotic ('r-ful') and non-rhotic ('r-less') dialects. Postvocalic /r/ will be a salient feature of those dialects which have it for speakers of dialects which do not. To a non-linguist from England, one of the most striking things about American or Scots English might well be 'that they say "r" when we don't'. An example of (2) – a difference of phonetic realisation only – would be the different pronunciations of the vowel of HOT in RP and American English: [ɒ] in RP, [ɑ] in many North American varieties.

While features which are points of contrast between two dialect systems appear to be the most salient for would-be imitators, they are also potentially the most difficult to copy correctly. British English speakers accommodating to North American pronunciation may be aware of rhotic pronunciations, but they actually acquire the postvocalic /r/ rather late (Trudgill 1986: 15,20). This is apparently because of the difficulty of knowing 'where to insert /r/'. Although most speakers in British society are also literate, and therefore have the advantage of knowing where /r/ occurs in writing, it is not clear that this is really a big help in flowing conversation, though it might be in very slow speech styles.

J.C. Wells (1973) reports on a study which is closely related to the concerns of this book. He studied the adaptations which adult Jamaicans made to accommodate their speech to LE – the reverse of what happens when young Black speakers of LE try to adapt their speech to the patterns of JC. Most of his informants had spent at least four years in Britain, and had left Jamaica after the age of sixteen (pp. 47–8). None had spent less than nine years in Jamaica before leaving, so that all had learnt their first language there. They are therefore not strictly comparable to the second generation London Caribbeans of this book. However, Wells's findings are certainly relevant. He found that his respondents were successful in emulating LE pronunciation where the adaptation involved 'phonetic modification of a particular phonological item (the vowel sounds in *face* and *nose*)'. They were less successful 'where it was a question of altering the distributional restraints on their phonology (the (r)-variables' – in this case, /r/-dropping rather than /r/-insertion, as required of British English speakers acquiring a North American accent. They were even more unsuccessful 'where it was a question of splitting a phonological item' (thus acquiring a contrast between *beer* and *bear*, which are pronounced alike in JC). Wells concludes that 'adolescents and adults, faced with a new linguistic environment, can adapt their speech to a certain extent by modifying the phonetic realisation of their phonemes; but they do not on the whole succeed in acquiring new phonological oppositions or in altering the distributional constraints on their phonology' (Wells 1973: 118).

Grammatical accommodation

Most of the preceding discussion deals with accommodation and adaptation at the phonological level. Sociolinguists working in the variationist paradigm have concentrated on studying phonological variation, and it is doubtful whether variationist techniques can be applied to grammatical variation at all. (For discussion, see Lavandera 1978; Romaine 1982: 31–7.) Nevertheless, we can assume that when speakers of two different varieties of a language come into contact, some sort of *grammatical* accommodation takes place.

Harris (1984) shows that even two varieties which are held *by their own speech communities* to be related dialects may actually have very different underlying grammatical systems: 'deep-seated structural divergences [may] exist between varieties which are intuitively felt to be dialects of the same language' (Harris 1984: 304). Speakers of Hiberno-English (one variety of English used in Ireland) are under increasing pressure to modify their language in the direction of Standard English, which is the prestige norm in Ireland. There is an obvious parallel with 'decreolisation', where a 'non-standard' variety is modified to become closer to the standard. However, as Harris shows, the underlying grammatical differences between the two 'dialects', HE and SE, are not trivial. The HE system of tense/aspect (like the JC one) is fundamentally different from that of SE. The native speaker of HE, trying to 'accommodate' to SE, is faced with trying to reconcile two incompatible systems. This means that in some cases, the HE speaker must 'lose' or neutralise a contrast which is normally expressed in HE. More difficult is the case where the HE speaker must learn to make a distinction which has to be expressed in SE but is not present in HE; the speaker must learn to 'split a category' as in the case of *beer* and *bear* mentioned above.

The Standard English distinction between past anterior ('then time'), marked by the preterite ('I saw' etc.) and indefinite present anterior, marked by the perfect ('I have seen' etc.) is not made in Hiberno-English. Harris demonstrates that 'some HE speakers show evidence of having acquired the standard perfect *form* but less than complete control over its *function*.' Such speakers may make overgeneralisations which are not appropriate *either* as HE or as SE, for example: 'I've done a course two years ago' (Harris 1984: 315). Thus it appears that the acquisition of the grammar of a new variety of 'the same' language is subject to the same difficulties and may lead to the same types of 'error' and inconsistency as the acquisition of its phonology.

Salience and social value

Phonological contrasts and phonetic differences may be important factors affecting accommodation but they are not the whole story. The *social* value attached to a salient feature – in particular, if it is part of a stereotype – may be important in determining whether or not it is accommodated to. For example, Trudgill (1986: 18) draws attention to the reluctance of North of England speakers, for whom a long /aː/ in *dance* is part of the Southern stereotype, to accommodate to this vowel, even though it is one that already exists in their system in words like *half* and *dark*. This he attributes to a resistance on the part of Northerners to adapt their speech towards a recognised stereotype, although they will happily adapt other vowels which carry less social significance. Hence the social value of a salient feature, in terms of its associated stereotype, may act as a brake on accommodation where a speaker is concerned with preserving his/her own identity, but may *promote* accommodation where the speaker is eager to identify with the other-dialect speakers.

Constructing 'Jamaican'

How does this relate to speakers of 'London Jamaican'? We have already seen several speakers – Susan, Stephen and Joan – whose 'Patois' seems to consist of a larger or smaller number of adaptations of LE in the direction of JC. Strongly stereotypical Creole features should be salient *and* positively valued as a symbol of identity, so we would expect these particular features of Creole to be accommodated to by everyone who attempts to engage in 'chattin' Patois'. However, all speakers will be constrained by limits on what is learnable in their given situation. If this is a correct description of what is happening, we would expect speakers' language behaviour to be characterised by:

(1) *incomplete adaptation* – since not all features of JC would be sufficiently salient to be 'noticeable' for the purposes of adaptation, some of these would 'slip through' and would fail to be adapted

(2) *inconsistency* – due to possible learning or memory constraints, or perhaps for other reasons not well understood, some adaptations would be made haphazardly, so that the same item might appear sometimes in its LE variant, sometimes in its JC form

(3) *misadaptation* – where the systems of JC and LE differ in such a way that adapting correctly requires recognising a contrast that exists in JC but not in LE, we would expect LE speakers to 'get it wrong' some of the time, creating forms which are *neither* the target (JC) nor LE.

In fact, we find all three of these in the 'Patois' of my informants.

Incomplete adaptation

It is difficult to separate incomplete adaptation from inconsistency, especially as both vary from speaker to speaker. We have seen that there are a large number of points of difference between JC and LE; yet Joan, in her conversation with Carol, adapts to only three or four of them. Other speakers adapt to far more, perhaps to most of them, at one time or another. However, there is one vowel sound which seems to undergo adaptation less than the others: this is the STRUT vowel [P3], which is [ʌ] in LE but [ɔ] in JC. Susan did not use the JC vowel in STRUT words at all. Stephen was inconsistent, using the JC variant only three times, and the LE form much more often. Joan also uses it inconsistently, having it in *but* but not in *rubbish* in the same line. Carol uses it consistently.

It would be foolish to make a strong claim about the salience of the JC STRUT vowel for LE speakers on the strength of limited data like this, but it does appear that for some speakers, this point of difference between LE and JC falls below a 'salience threshold' which leads it to be ignored for adaptation purposes, while for other speakers it is salient enough to be adapted, but not consistently. It may be significant that the only speaker who *never* adapts the STRUT vowel is the white speaker, Susan.[1]

Inconsistency

We have already seen several examples of inconsistency in adaptation. There is one caveat here. I have argued that speakers who use Creole in conversation usually are able to switch strategically between LE and what, *for that speaker*, counts as Creole or Patois. That speaker's 'Patois', however, will also be constructed as a series of adaptations from LE, except in relatively rare cases where the speaker has a genuinely native command of the Creole. Such speaker's 'Patois' will therefore be subject to incomplete adaptation, inconsistency and misadaptation, but this is only significant if the target language of that utterance is Creole. If the speaker has actually switched to LE, there is *intentionally* no adaptation. What may appear to be inconsistencies may, in fact, be code switches. Sometimes, however, we can identify 'failures to adapt' which stick out by virtue of the fact that everything around them is successfully adapted, for example:

> You na [G15] go run [P3] **frough** (=[fɹuː]) dis dyam brick wall [P4]
> 'You're not going to run through this damn brick wall!'
> (JC 'through' = [tɹuː])

Misadaptation

Susan's use of /r/ at the end of *Jamaica* is a classic example of misadaptation (also called 'hypercorrection', 'hyperadaptation').

Knowing that /r/ occurs word-finally in JC in many words which end in [ə] or [a] in LE, she applies her /r/-insertion rule too widely, and in this case, in a word where it should not apply. Susan happens to be a white speaker, but this is not the only case of misadaptation: black speakers do it as well, although rarely. For example, one boy – in other respects a very fluent and convincing Creole speaker – said:

> You call dem law [lʊɒɹ] but dey break de law [lʊɒɹ]
> 'You call them law, but they break the law!'

In this sentence, *all* the vowel and consonant sounds were adapted to JC, in *call* [P4], *but* [P3] and the initial TH of *them, they* and *the*. However, the /r/ in *law* is a misadaptation. The JC pronunciation is [la:] – in other words, it belongs to the lexical set of THOUGHT, not NORTH.

It is easy to see how the misadaptation came about. In LE, *sore* [sɔə] rhymes with *law* [lɔə] (Wells 1982: 310), while *saw* and *lore* are homophones of these, respectively. On the other hand, JC *sore* is /soːr/, while *saw* is /saː/. Adapting LE to JC in this case means distinguishing those lexical items which historically end in /r/ from those which do not. In this case, the speaker made the wrong choice and produced a form which is neither LE nor JC, though the target was certainly JC. Notice also that the choice the speaker made was the one which would make his Creole seem maximally *different* from LE: i.e., would reinforce the stereotype of Creole as a different system.

The above examples all relate to phonology, but there are examples of mis-adaptation from the grammar as well. One relatively common type of mis-adaptation involves doing 'Subject/Auxiliary inversion' [G20] with a past tense marked by *did*. Since the tense markers in JC are not verbs, but invariant particles, there are no *syntactic* grounds for identifying British English *did* (the past tense of *do*) with Creole *did* (a past tense marker, but *not* the past tense of *do*, which would be *en, bin* or *did do*). Some London speakers make this identification, however, with results like

> Did him give you what you a look for?
> What time did unu (you-plural) reach home?

Other aspects of the grammar and phonology of these sentences (from different speakers) make it clear that they are *intended* to be 'Patois'. However, neither would be acceptable as JC, where the following would be expected:

Him did give you what you a look for?
What time unu did reach home?

There are some examples which show that we are really dealing with adaptations of LE, and that speakers may not even be conscious of corresponding lexical items in JC. The 'THink/boTHer' phonological feature [P17] shows a three-way contrast: JC /tri:/, JSE/BSE /θri:/, LE /fri:/ 'three'. J.C. Wells (1982: 328) regards /f/ and /θ/ as underlyingly different for all London speakers, since 'if [θ] and [f] were stylistic alternatives realising the same underlying phoneme /f/ in all cases, we should have frequent hypercorrections such as *[θaɪv] or [θaɪð] *five*' but these are virtually unknown. Similarly for the voiced counterparts of /t θ f/, namely /d ð v/.

However, there are several examples from different speakers of [f] or [v] in places where JC has /t/ or /d/. One girl talked about [bava bu:t] 'bovver boots', a type of heavy boot associated (in the past at least) with toughness and aggression. The name of the boot is from the word 'bother', which in LE can have the meaning 'violence'. The corresponding Jamaican word is [bada], with RP /ð/ → /d/, but this is not the adaptation made by the speaker, who bases her adaptation on the London form 'bovver' ([bɒvə]). This is especially interesting because Adelman (1976: 86) cites a distinctive use of *bovver* (as opposed to *bother*) in teenage argot: 'I had a little bother', e.g. trouble starting the car, vs. 'I had a little bovver', i.e. was involved in a fight (Adelman 1976: 86, cited in Romaine 1984: 189). Other similar instances are /fru:/ 'through', /bref/ 'breath'.

So at least some speakers fail to adapt these lexical items successfully to their JC form. A likely explanation would be that correct adaptation on the basis of the *LE* form requires the speaker to 'split' /f/, thus: LE [fʊt], JC [fʊt] 'foot', but LE [fɪŋk], JC [tɪŋk] 'think'. Since, as J.C. Wells argues, /f/ and /θ/ seem to be underlyingly distinct phonemes for LE speakers (including, presumably, Caribbeans), this suggests that the phonological adapta tions from LE are based on the *surface* realisation of the sound in question, i.e. its actual realisation as [f], rather than the underlying representation as /f/ or /θ/.

Successful adaptation

In the last section we saw three ways in which speakers can *miss* their target of JC. On the other side of the coin, we would expect that those features of the Creole which (a) are salient and (b) do not present the speaker with any special difficulties of the sort involved in /r/-insertion, will be *successfully* imitated most of the time. In this category we might expect to find phonological and grammatical features which are sufficiently different from British English to be salient, but which do not involve, in J.C. Wells's terms, 'altering the distributional restraints on their phonology' or 'splitting a phonological item' (i.e. acquiring a new contrast).

There are some candidates for 'highly imitable' features of this sort. One phonological variable that meets this description is the JC pronunciation of the FACE and GOAT vowels [P5,P6]. Looking at our four speakers: Susan, Stephen, Carol and Joan, we find that all of them use a form phonetically different from the LE/RP sound. Susan, Carol and Joan use the basilectal [iɛ]/[ʊɔ̈], while Stephen uses [e:]/[o:] – though this may be due to Eastern Caribbean (St Vincentian) influence. In Joan's case, this is one of the few phonological adaptations which she makes. The FACE vowel seems to be part of the stereotype – witness the way one speaker introduced himself on the tape (W is of Barbadian parentage, E Jamaican):

W   My name is Wayne [weən] I come from Spain [speən] and it
     always rain [ɹeən] in de train [tɹeən]
E   Backside!
     [general laughter]

This is not Wayne's normal speech style, but 'fooling about', as evidenced by E's response ('backside' = 'rubbish', though much less polite) and the laughter of all four people in the room.

A possible candidate for a grammatical feature in this category is the Creole past tense. This takes two different forms: the base form of the verb without any preverbal marker ([G4]) and a preverbal marker (which in Jamaica may be *en* or *ben*, but in Britain is nearly always *did*) ([G6]). Although the two forms are almost certainly *not* interchangeable in JC, having different functions, both are used for past actions and map broadly on to the British English simple past. They are also 'easy' to imitate in *form* though possibly not in *use*: one requires the *omission* of past tense morphology (*run* not *ran, look* not *looked*), the other requires only the insertion of the word *did* which already exists in LE. This may account for its use even by white speakers like Susan, and 'minimal' black Creole speakers like Joan: though whether their use of these forms would be judged correct by JC speakers is difficult to say. [2]

From this discussion of London Creole we turn now to look at the London *English* of my informants in the next chapter.

Notes

1. This finding is at variance with the findings reported by Edwards (1986). Her data from Dudley, West Midlands, shows that this is one of the *first* Creole features adapted to. All 45 of her informants adapted this vowel.
2. Edwards (1986) found that while the simple past was acquired early by her Dudley informants, the past marked with *did*, etc. was acquired much later.

5 . . . or Black London English?

Is there a distinctive form of *English* spoken by black people in London?

It is not unusual to find, within a larger speech community such as London or New York, particular sub-communities with their own distinctive variety of the common language. It is reasonable to ask whether the Caribbean community in London has such a distinctive variety of English, characterised by features of accent, grammar or vocabulary which are closely identified with members of that community only.

Unfortunately, it is not possible to give a very clear answer to this. To begin with, there is a dearth of studies of LE. While it is well recognised that London has its own distinctive speech, characterised by features of accent and grammar in particular, there are surprisingly few 'dialect' studies of London (in contrast with, for example, areas more traditionally thought of as using 'dialect', such as Lancashire or Norfolk). The majority of studies which have been undertaken have been phonetic: see Wells (1982) for bibliography. To complicate matters, it is also clear that 'LE' is not a single homogenous dialect, but varies considerably – though perhaps too subtly for outsiders to notice – from district to district. This aspect of London speech has also been largely neglected by researchers.

In view of what I have said above, it is not surprising that no studies have been undertaken specifically to determine whether black London speech is distinctive from the LE of other groups. It is apparent that any differences must be very small, and may not be noticeable to people from outside London at all. (The stereotype of the London-born Caribbean, both for Caribbeans and others, involves having a marked LE accent.) What we can say is that Caribbean usages have spread outwards beyond the Caribbean community itself, so that there are a number of expressions of Caribbean origin now in use in London both within and outside the black community. Speakers from outside the black community, however, may not have any idea of the origin of these expressions, while even those within the black community may not realise their Caribbean connections.

This suggests that the notion of a distinctive variety restricted *solely* to Londoners of Caribbean ethnic origin may be simplistic. Hewitt (1989), for example, accepts that the speech of black adolescents shows influences from Creole but asserts that the *same* influences can be seen in white adolescents' English in certain areas:

> the English of many black youngsters also itself displayed evidence of Creole influence beyond those stretches that might be plainly treated as switches. Lexical and grammatical forms often entered in from Creole sources, although which forms, where they appeared, and how frequently, varied greatly from speaker to speaker. (Hewitt 1989: 138)

But he goes on to say:

> while such Creole influences may have been more evident and highly focused (Le Page 1975) in the speech of black youngsters, they were by no means restricted to black speakers but were to varying degrees evident also in the speech of white and ethnic minority youth other than Afro-Caribbean from the same localities. (p. 139)

So rather than use the other terms which have been suggested to describe this variety, such as 'black Cockney', 'black London English', 'British Black English', which suggest a specifically *black* 'ethnolect', Hewitt prefers to talk of the 'local multi-racial vernacular'. While Hewitt's decision to use this term is based *partly* on his belief that there is no characteristic variety of English used *solely* by ethnic Caribbeans, it is also motivated by the lack of *symbolic* meaning attached to this variety:

it was not the case that the London English of young blacks took on any specialized symbolic meaning of race or ethnicity. Neither was it manipulated or controlled for specific stylistic effects concerned with those aspects. Rather, it was the site of low-key, social symbolic renovation, wherein ethnicity was, if anything, deconstructed and a new *ethnically mixed* 'community English' created from the fragments. (Hewitt 1989: 139)

On Hewitt's account, it is *Creole* which carries the symbolic values of ethnicity and culture, for both its black and white speakers, while the 'multi-racial vernacular' serves as a common community language, the 'ordinary English' of the symbolic 'Creole'/'ordinary English' dichotomy. There is plenty of evidence of Caribbean influence on the speech of London adolescents, though there has been little systematic study in this area. Hewitt's 'multi-racial vernacular' certainly exists, but it is not the whole story. Creolisms do not enter the language of the wider community all at once, directly from Creole. Most of them must first pass through a stage of being used within LE by black speakers, before being taken up by the LE speaking community as a whole. Since a number of factors determine whether a form of expression will be taken up into popular speech, and somewhat different factors will operate within and outside the black community, not all Creole forms used by black speakers will achieve wider currency, though some will.

In the next few sections I will look at the characteristics of LE as used by the black community, with respect to vocabulary, grammar and accent.

Vocabulary

Individual words are probably the most 'mobile' parts of a language, so it should come as no surprise that words of Creole origin are used by blacks *and* whites within LE. Hewitt (1986: 129) found 'some thirty distinctly Creole lexical items' in the speech of white adolescents in an area of high Caribbean population. Some of the words listed by Hewitt are in fact just special *uses* of existing British English words, which are given new meaning within the youth culture: e.g. *hard, soff (soft), dread, star, sweet*. Some, including *soff, tief, cruff* are identifiable as of Creole origin by virtue of their pronunciation, (and in the case of *tief* also by its use as a verb rather than a noun) which distinguishes them from their Standard counterparts *soft*, *thief*, *scruff(y)*, which have no special meaning within youth culture. Others, like *bambaclaht* and *renk* are Creole items without counterparts in Standard English.

Outside the realm of youth culture, however, there are words of Caribbean origin which may be 'anglicised' or adapted to LE phonological patterns by black speakers when using LE. Examples include *duppy* (LE [dʌpɪi] JC [dɒpɪ]) 'ghost', *crablouse* (LE [kɹæblʌʊs] JC [kɹablɒus]) 'type of louse', *picky-picky* (LE [pɪkɪipɪkɪi] JC [pɪkɪpɪkɪ]) 'frizzy, like peppercorn hair'. Although these words refer to particularly Caribbean concepts, they can be treated by speakers as words of ordinary (i.e. London) English in terms of their pronunciation.

Creole words can thus follow either of two routes into LE: (1) with their Creole pronunciation intact, as a badge of their ethnic origin and distinctness from Standard English words of the same form, or (2) in 'anglicised' form, conforming to the pronunciation rules of LE. Words in the first category seem inherently more likely to succeed as part of the vocabulary of youth culture by virtue of their being marked from the start as *oppositional* to mainstream culture through their Creole pronunciation, and by this route to enter the 'multi-racial vernacular'. Words in category (2) seem to be confined to black speakers, though this remains at this stage an untested observation.

Grammar

Many black speakers show occasional signs of Creole influence on grammar when speaking otherwise 'ordinary' LE although there are none which *invariably* appear in the speech of black Londoners. It is difficult to say what kind of status these Creole grammatical features have in the LE of individuals. They are clearly not 'mistakes' from the point of view of their speakers, although to a hearer who knows nothing of Creole they may sound very odd. They are also not confined to the black community: Hewitt (1986: 190–2) discusses at length the speech of a white boy which shows numerous Creole grammatical influences while remaining basically LE. In the case of the white boy, we can rule out the possibility of 'mother-tongue' interference because his first exposure to Creole was almost certainly rather late in life and too late to 'interfere' with his acquisition of LE. In the case of black speakers, because LE is almost certainly their dominant language, though they may have been exposed to Creole first; at any rate, the possibility that these occasional 'Creolisms' are due to a carry-over from the 'mother tongue' remains doubtful and unproven.

Furthermore, these Creole features of grammar do not appear to carry any particular symbolic value either (see the quote from Hewitt above) and the contexts in which they occur do not make them look like code switches. While individual speakers may be quite consistent in using these features, none of them is universal and no systematic research has been done to show how widespread they may be. I will just discuss a handful of the most common here.

1. Seh ('say') = 'that'

JC *seh* [sɛ] is used, according to Cassidy and Le Page (1980: 396):

> After verbs such as *think, know, believe, suppose, see* or others involving communication, as, *tell, hear, promise*, introducing the object clause: virtually equivalent to *that*. (Sometimes *that* is used redundantly after it.)

JC *seh* has a long history, almost certainly originating from a verb (which later became reanalysed as a complementiser corresponding to 'that') in one of the West African languages of the Kwa group. Kwa languages were an important influence on the Caribbean Creoles at the time of their formation (and subsequently while slaves continued to be imported from West Africa). Several other Creoles have a complementiser which, like *seh* is verbal in origin: for example Sranan *taki* from English *talk*, which is also usually translated *that* in this context.

In the LE of black speakers we find examples like:

> we like to win, but if we lose, we know *seh* we tried, all of us tried

> a all whi%e jury found out *seh* 'e was guilty

sometimes fings 'appen, right, and you know _seh_ really an' truly it ain't gonna work out

The above examples came from three different speakers from East London, but I have one example from South East London as well. It is remarkable that speakers use this function word, which itself seems to carry no symbolic meaning, and offers no advantage in expressive terms over the ordinary LE _that_. When it is used, it is used in accordance with the rules of JC. Thus while it may introduce an object clause, as in the above examples, sentences like the one below, where it introduces a subject clause, are not found:

* _seh_ she came to your party doesn't mean she likes you

Thus although _seh_ is equivalent to _that_ in some contexts, we do not have a simple case of replacing a British English lexical item with a Creole one. The rules governing the use of _seh_ are different from those which apply to _that_.

Cassidy and Le Page say that _seh_ is 'never pronounced like English say', always having the short open [ɛ] vowel also found in JC take and _make_, but when used in LE it sometimes _does_ seem to have the diphthong of LE _say_. This suggests that its pronunciation has been 'anglicised' even though its Creole function has been retained.

2. Stay

Here again, a lexical item shared with British English is involved but its _use_ is as in Creole. In JC, _stay_ [stiɛ] is used as a copular verb instead of _be_ where the state is ongoing or permanent. This is the way it is used in the following example, but the _pronunciation_ of the word is exactly as in LE:

You know how white people stay.
'You know how white people are.'

3. Subject and object pronouns

The JC pronouns _mi_ and _dem_ are derived historically from the English object pronouns _me_ and _them_ although in JC they may be used as subjects. Some black speakers carry this use over into English:

> me's all for the Argentinians bombing them up
> me say 'I agree with you'

Note the alternation between 'me' and 'I' in the second example.

Accent

Black Londoners for the most part sound *very* London. But do they also sound identifiably black? It seems that in some cases the answer is yes, even though no characteristic elements of *segmental* phonology have been found which distinguish black Londoners' speech from that of other Londoners. Hewitt (1989: 139), for example, writes: 'most locals could more or less accurately tell the race of an unseen adolescent speaker – where non-locals or at least those unfamiliar with inner-London speech might report knowing only that Cockney was being spoken.'

There has to date been no detailed investigation of the pronunciation of black native speakers of LE: in fact there have been few recent studies of LE pronunciation. This makes it hard to claim categorically that there are no characteristically 'black' features which might identify speakers as ethnic Caribbeans. However, there are no obvious candidates for such features. It would not be surprising, though, if there were differences between the London Englishes spoken by black and white Londoners, given the different linguistic background of most black speakers of LE. Trudgill (1986: 36–7) reports research which shows that certain vowel distinctions in Norwich English are unlikely to be correctly acquired even by children *born* in Norwich, unless their parents were also born there. Trudgill writes:

> speakers are not capable of acquiring the correct underlying phonological distinction unless they are exposed to it from the very beginning, before they themselves have even begun to speak. Exposure to it in the speech of their peers from the age of four or five is, surprising as this may seem, not sufficient.

Trudgill's informants grew up in Norwich at a time when the city was expanding to accommodate many incomers from surrounding localities and from London: the resulting linguistic situation may well have been characterised by diffuse norms which allowed 'outsiders', including those born in Norwich to parents from elsewhere, to 'get away with' an imperfect knowledge of the Norwich dialect. Such a description would presumably fit London as well, especially the areas of Caribbean settlement.

Under these circumstances, *some* differences between black and white London speech are to be expected. As in the case of grammar, sporadic 'creolisms' in pronunciation can be heard in the speech of some of my informants. These often involve vowel sounds having their Creole rather than their expected London pronunciations. However, they are probably too infrequent to provide hearers with cues to ethnicity.

Another possible locus of difference between black and white speech is in *voice setting*. Laver (1991) describes these as 'the way in which the speaker "sets" his muscular vocal apparatus for speaking'. These include *voice quality settings* – 'habitual tendencies towards constricting (or expanding) the tract at some particular point along its length', and *voice-dynamic settings* which include (habitual ranges of) pitch and loudness (Laver 1991: 247). Laver goes on:

> Because voice settings are under potential muscular control, they are learnable and imitable. The adoption of a particular voice setting often acts as an individuating marker, when its use is idiosyncratic to a particular speaker. But voice settings often form part of the typical verbal performance of particular regional accents, and can thus also act as social markers. (Laver 1991: 247)

Furthermore, different voice settings typically characterise different languages, and these settings may carry over into the pronunciation of a second language (Laver 1991: 248). So voice settings typical of Creole could still, in theory, characterise the speech even of the younger generation of the Caribbean community in London. Unfortunately, no systematic research has been done to determine the typical voice settings of speakers of Caribbean Creoles or of members of the Caribbean community in Britain. The idea that Caribbean English in Britain has its own characteristic voice setting therefore remains just a guess.

In order to discover whether voice setting and other factors might give hearers clues to a speaker's ethnicity, I asked 43 East

London children aged about 14 to listen to 12 short stretches of speech on tape and fill in a questionnaire. The children were members of two classes at a secondary school in Leytonstone, London E11. In response to a question about their own ethnicity, 12 answered that they were 'black' or 'West Indian', and 22 'white' or 'Anglo-Saxon'. Ten others either gave no answer or did not fall into either of these groups. These (and two incomplete questionnaires) have been excluded from consideration here.

The extracts on tape represented speakers of different ages, sexes and 'styles', i.e. 'Creole' vs. 'LE'. The pupils were allowed to think that they were listening to the voices of 12 different speakers, but actually there were only 9. All but one of them were black. Four were aged twelve or thirteen, 4 were aged fifteen or sixteen, and one, a man born in Jamaica, was aged thirty-five–forty. There were 4 female and 5 male speakers. Three of the speakers appeared twice in different 'guises', once speaking LE, once speaking Creole or something close to it. This is the classical 'matched guise' technique developed by Lambert, Giles and others (see Lambert et al. 1960; Giles and Powesland 1975) with the difference that the extracts on tape were from genuine conversational data and were therefore not standardised. This led to a problem in at least one case described below, where there was a contextual clue to the speaker's ethnicity. Other such clues may have gone unnoticed by the researcher, though responded to by the subjects.

None of the pupils seemed to guess that they had heard the same speaker more than once. On the questionnaire form, the pupils were asked to guess the age and sex of each speaker, his or her background, and where he or she came from. They were asked to give a 'confidence rating' on a scale from 1 to 3 for their answer (1 being least and 3 being most confident). There was also a space for comments on the speaker's language. They were then asked to listen to the voices a second time and say whether each was 'black, white or other', giving a confidence rating. The task was 'forced' in that the respondents were not allowed to answer 'impossible to say' to the question about the speaker's race, but had to opt for one of the three possibilities, although they could give this the lowest confidence rating. The results are shown in part in Table 5.1.

Table 5.1

Speaker	Age	Sex	Ethnic group	Syntax	Phonology	'Black' group % correct (a)	'White' group % correct (a)
1	12	F	Caribbean	LE	LE	8 (3.0)	9 (3.0)
2	12	F	White	JC	JC	18 (1.5)	27 (2.7)
3	12	F	"	LE	LE	42 (1.4)	27 (2.2)
4	13	M	"	LE	LE	45 (1.7)	5 (3.0)
5	16	F	"	LE	LE	55 (2.3)	27 (2.3)
6	?35	M	"	JSE	JSE	64 (2.4)	14 (1.7)
7	(= 1)		"	JC	JC	67 (2.6)	81 (2.4)
8	(= 5)		Caribbean	JC	JC	91 (2.6)	73 (2.6)
9	15	M	"	LE	?LE	91 (2.7)	86 (2.4)
10	15	F	"	LE	?LE	100 (2.2)	100 (2.7)
11	(= 2)		White	LE	LE	100 (2.3)	81 (2.6)
12	16	M	Caribbean	JC	JC	100 (2.1)	100 (2.7)

Notes: (a) figure in brackets is mean confidence for the group who
        guessed speaker's ethnicity correctly.
        (b) LE = London English; JC = Jamaican Creole;
        JSE = Jamaican Standard English.

Overall, the group of pupils who identified themselves as
'black' or 'West Indian' were significantly better (p < 0.5) than
the group who identified themselves as 'white' or 'Anglo-Saxon'
at guessing the ethnicity of the speakers. The 'black' group were
correct 61.6 per cent of the time (over all 12 voices) and the
'white' group 52.5 per cent of the time. Both groups were about
equally confident of their judgements (mean confidence rating 2.6
for the black group's *correct* guesses, 2.5 for the white group's).

In fact, both groups did well in recognising black speakers
who used Creole syntactic and phonological features (speakers 7,
8 and 12) while both did badly when presented with a white
speaker using Creole syntax and phonology (speaker 2). The
same white speaker when using LE without Creole features
(speaker 11) was correctly recognised by all the 'black' group and
81 per cent of the 'white' group, both with high confidence (2.3
and 2.6 respectively). This suggests that the pre-eminent strategy
the subjects used to guess ethnicity was to make a simple correla-

tion between speech style and ethnicity: LE for white speakers, Creole for black speakers.

There were some differences between the groups, mainly in the recognition of black speakers who were *not* using Creole features of syntax or segmental phonology. Speakers in this category were numbers 1, 3, 4 and 5 who were on average correctly identified 36.4 per cent of the time by the 'black' group and 17.2 per cent of the time by the 'white' group. This difference is significant (p < 0.05); however, the two groups did not differ significantly in their ability to recognise speakers 1 and 3, whom they overwhelmingly failed to identify as black. There was also only a weakly significant difference between the groups in their recognition of speaker 5. However, the 'black' group was significantly better at recognising speaker 4 as black, although he used no distinctively Creole syntax or segmental phonology. I shall discuss this speaker further below.

Another significant difference between the groups was in their responses to speaker 6, an adult Jamaican speaking Jamaican Standard English with its characteristic accent, devoid of Creole features. The 'black' group were significantly better at recognising this speaker (p < 0.1); most of the 'white' group felt this speaker was Asian and assigned him to the 'other' category. It is reasonable to assume that this is because the stereotype of the educated Jamaican Standard speaker is one that is familiar to children of Caribbean background but is not generally recognised in the white community.

Both the 'black' and 'white' groups were very good at identifying speakers 9, 10, 11 and 12. Speaker 11 was the white girl who, as speaker 2 speaking Creole, convinced most of the listeners that she was black. Speaker 12 used Creole syntax *and* phonology and was judged to be black by the majority of respondents, just as they had judged Speaker 2 (= 11) to be black in her 'Creole' guise.

Speakers 9 and 10 are more interesting in that *neither* of them used Creole syntactic features or any of the segmental phonological features that are characteristic of Creole, or are identifiably part of the 'Patois' stereotype. Both of these boys were also Patois speakers, and had used Patois within the conversation from which the extracts were taken: but the extracts were chosen carefully to exclude any *obvious* 'Creolisms'. It seems that the listeners, both black and white, were able to home in on some as yet unidentified aspect of the phonology of these two adolescent boys which identified them as black.

We saw above that there was one other speaker who was generally correctly identified as black – but in this case, only by the *black* group. This was the preadolescent boy, speaker 4. One could hypothesise that there is some phonological clue to ethnicity in this speaker's speech which is apparent to members of the black community but not to others. This 'clue', whatever it is, may become more obvious in adolescence, so that older black males are readily identified by their speech even by *non*-members of the community, as in the case of speakers 9 and 10. In connection with speaker 4, it is interesting that those in the black group who correctly guessed his ethnicity did so with markedly less confidence than the average (mean confidence 1.7).

If there is really a divide of this type between preadolescent and adolescent boys, it would be reasonable to ask if the same is true of girls. Note that speaker 1 (aged twelve – preadolescent) was incorrectly judged to be white by nearly all respondents, but that the black group were slightly better than the white at identifying speaker 5 (aged sixteen – adolescent). This would be consistent with a hypothesis that the identifiable 'Creoleness' of black speech increases with age, and is more marked in boys than in girls. Speaker 3 appears to be a counter-example to this, in that the black group did better than the white group in guessing her to be black, although the difference was not statistically significant. The difference turns out, however, to be due to a contextual clue. Speaker 3 says she is good at sport and 'fastest in the Borough'. Since there was a belief among many black schoolchildren that the 'fastest in the Borough' would always be a black child, some made their assessment of ethnicity on this basis rather than a linguistic one. In this case, the confidence of the black group was rather low both for those who were right (mean confidence 1.4) and those who were wrong (mean confidence 1.7).

To sum up, it seems that some adolescent black boys are readily identified as such by features of their voice, both by other members of the black community and by outsiders. Preadolescent boys and girls of all ages are less identifiable as black, although their ethnicity may be 'guessable' for members of their own community. This is quite consistent with Hewitt's remark that 'most locals could more or less accurately tell the race of an unseen adolescent speaker' (see above).

A single experiment of this sort cannot provide a firm basis for any wide-ranging claims. However, it does suggest that there are recognisable 'black' voice characteristics which do not operate at the level of segmental phonology, but have to do with such factors as prosodic features, voice setting, and perhaps other elements which remain to be identified.

Agreement marking in black LE: *You know what I mean?*

Agreement markers are those utterance types – whether lexical items, sentences or sentence fragments – which are used in conversation to show agreement with a proposition. In Standard English they range from *uh-huh* and *yes* to the explicit *I agree with you*. There are many other options, of course, dependent on context.

Agreement marking is the locus of an interesting difference between JC and Creole-influenced LE on the one hand, and non-Creole-influenced varieties of British English on the other. The details are given in Sebba and Tate (1986), and what follows is a summary.

In most varieties of British English, *you know what I mean?* and *you know?* are used by parties in a conversation to *elicit* agreement, as in the following (made up) example:

(1)   A: I can't make head nor tail of this, you know what I mean?
       B: Yeah.

Alternatives to B's 'yeah' might be: 'I know', 'I know what you mean', 'Exactly', 'I sure do', etc. – all of which respond to the question form of A's 'you know what I mean?' However, it can be argued that A's 'you know what I mean?' is not really a question, though it has the form of a question. It is actually intended to elicit an agreement – in other words, to get confirmation of B's support for what A has said. B's possible responses listed above, while overtly responding to the question 'you know what I mean?' are actually *heard* by parties to the conversation as supporting A's proposition, 'I can't make head nor tail of this'.

In the speech of many young black Londoners, exchanges like the following take place:

(2) A: It was a wicked party, man!
     B: You know what I mean!

or, perhaps more frequently

(3) A: It was a wicked party, man!
     B: You know!

It can easily be shown that 'you know what I mean!' and 'you know!' in this case cannot be *eliciting* an agreement. The only proposition with which they *could* be eliciting an agreement is that made by A: but it does not make sense for B to elicit an agreement with A's proposition. It is clear from the context of such pairs that in every case where the second speaker responds to a proposition of the first speaker with 'you know what I mean!' or 'you know!', the second speaker is in fact *agreeing* with the first. In pairs of this type, the work being done by 'you know what I mean' and 'you know' is fundamentally different from the work they are doing in the more Standard sort of exchange in (1). In short, 'you know what I mean' has gone from being an agreement-seeker to being a *marker* of agreement in conversation.

This change of function is one which could potentially have severe consequences for understanding. A speaker for whom 'you know what I mean?' is only an agreement-seeker may not understand a speaker who uses it to *mark* agreement. To such a person exchanges like (2) and (3) may seem quite bizarre. The agreement marking use of 'you know what I mean?' seems to be confined to people under the age of about 30, which makes it likely that misunderstandings, if they occur, will be inter-generational.

What is particularly interesting about the agreement-marking 'you know what I mean' is that it is possible – anecdotally, and rather impressionistically – to trace its recent history in London. Agreement-marking 'you know what I mean' and 'you know' are well-established in JC (see Sebba and Tate 1986) but have never been reported before the 1980s in any type of British English in Britain. It seems certain that they first found their way from the Creole of the first generation Caribbean migrants into the LE of the second generation, where they occur very frequently. From this community they have spread out and have now become a part of LE for adolescents and children of all races, though perhaps (no research has been done to my knowledge) only in areas where there is significant contact between the black and white communities.

The case of 'you know what I mean' is especially interesting because it does not fall into any of the traditional categories of lexis, grammar or phonology. Instead it involves a shift in function in an *interactional* category, and it is exactly here – in the interactions between individuals – that we would expect to see most clearly the results of inter-ethnic contact. And so we do, for the agreement-marking use of 'you know what I mean' has spread from the Caribbean community to the wider London community where presumably very few are aware of its Caribbean origins. Thus, perhaps, is Hewitt's 'multi-racial vernacular' made a reality.

Conclusions

Chapters 4 and 5 demonstrate that the linguistic repertoire of many young black Londoners and some young whites can be analysed in terms of two main varieties, Creole/'Patois' on the one hand and 'ordinary' English on the other. This distinction is preserved even by those whose real command of Creole is quite limited. On the Creole side, speakers focus on JC, irrespective of their ethnic origins. For these speakers, 'ordinary English' means London English, though it is not identical with the LE of earlier generations.

This 'Creole-influenced' variety of LE shows occasional grammatical and phonological influences of Creole and has also undergone some restructuring at the *interactional* level in the direction of Creole. It is probably not confined to black speakers alone, but is spoken to varying degrees by young white people. In the case of one interactional variable, the agreement-marking 'you know what I mean', it seems fairly certain that this originated in the Caribbean community and has spread outwards to the wider community of LE speakers. It thus becomes difficult to identify a specifically *black* LE, although there seem to be certain features of accent which community members are able to use to identify unseen speakers as black.

From dealing in the last few chapters with the language of individuals, we now turn, in Chapter 6, to a discussion of how language is used within Caribbean families in London.

6 Language within the Family

Monolingual families may seem all alike (see Chapter 7 for a refutation of this!), but multilingual families are each multilingual after their own fashion. At least, there is likely to be considerable diversity in the behaviour of London families of Caribbean origin, since each individual in each of the two, three or four generations in one family may have differing degrees of linguistic and cultural contact with the Caribbean.

What I have to report here are *observations* of the behaviour of a number of families who agreed to make recordings in the context of the research project described in my Introduction. The findings for one family may be generalisable to others, but where the circumstances of each family are different, linguistic behaviour may be different too.

Patterns of language use and maintenance

The concept of *domain* is central to the diglossic view of bilingualism that was dominant in studies of bilingual communities until recently: see Martin-Jones (1991) for a critical appraisal of this approach. Martin-Jones (1991: 50) writes:

> The main tenet of the diglossia model (Fishman 1967; 1980) is that the languages of the bilingual communities are functionally differentiated. They are associated with distinct domains of use. Diglossia refers to the community norms for language allocation across domains. Language use among individual bilinguals is seen as being governed by these norms.

Research within this paradigm is usually focused on finding out which language is used in which domain by particular subgroups of speakers – for example, different generations within one community; in Fishman's famous phrase, 'who speaks what language to whom and when?' (1965).

Generation has a significant role in this paradigm because in many bilingual communities, the first generation who settled in Britain from abroad were native speakers of a language very unlike English and had had little or no exposure to English. This was particularly true for some groups, for example women in some Muslim communities. The use of English was thus significantly more restricted in the first generation than in the second generation, who had generally attended British schools and often had a native-like command of British English. Researchers tended to focus on the generation differences, in particular with respect to the possible decline in use of the mother tongue among second-generation speakers in some domains, and differential use of mother-tongue and English in others. For example, this is the pattern that emerges from studies of Urdu speakers in Britain described by Khan (1991), who writes:

> Urdu thus emerges as having greater currency for first-generation than second-generation speakers. There are indications of a shift towards the use of English, which is least marked in domains outside [*sic*] the home and in the case of interactions between parents and grandparents but particularly noticeable in conversations with siblings. (Khan 1991: 133)

If this kind of picture were to apply to the London Caribbean community, we should expect to find a pattern where Creole was used between members of the first generation and by them to their children. The children would use London English and Creole among themselves, and mainly Creole to their parents. Furthermore, there would be 'domains' where Creole and English could properly be used by those who speak them: Creole in the family and in informal situations, English within the public domain outside the family and even within the family on formal occasions.

The influence of the 'diglossia' paradigm is apparent in the 'reported pattern of dialect selection' represented as a tree diagram in Sutcliffe (1982a: 148). Adolescent speakers are shown as making a choice between 'English' and 'Jamaican Creole' on the basis of domain (home/school; playground/classroom), interlocutor (white/black) and interaction type (+/- conflict). However, Sutcliffe does not specify the details of language choice within the home, saying only that 'complicated factors' are involved. Sutcliffe adds (p. 149):

> The girls' collective perception of usage at home was summed up in the comment '*plien* [plain] English – and sometimes Jamaican' . . . Various happenings that could bring about a shift into Creole were mentioned, including 'talking to my Grandma about some of these teachers'. But by and large the consensus was that children tended to use English at home, while parents very often used 'Jamaican', especially when old friends came visiting.

Unfortunately, though this description tells part of the truth, it is greatly oversimplified. Sutcliffe remarks that his diagram is 'incomplete even within its own simple terms of reference' (1982a: 149). More generally, the 'diglossia' paradigm tends to emphasise linguistic behaviour in terms of community norms rather than individual interactions which are *orientated to* those norms in a general way. This leads to oversimplification, at least when applied to the Caribbean community in London. The simplifications begin with the assumption that 'Creole' is the language of the parents' generation. This can only be true for those speakers who are more or less monostylistic and 'basilectal': in other words, those whose repertoire is confined to a variety of Creole which is almost maximally different from Standard English. In Jamaica and other parts of the Caribbean such speakers will be found only in the lowest socioeconomic classes, those whose education and social contacts have hardly brought them into contact with Standard English at all. Furthermore, these individuals would have to have remained more or less monostylistic even *after* their arrival in Britain and their exposure to various types of British English, over periods of up to thirty years.

Such people are likely to be a very small proportion of the first generation Caribbean community in London. The Caribbeans who came to London in the main waves of migration in the 1950s and early 1960s were not on the whole from the lowest social classes, although 'the employment made available to West Indians was mainly menial and often of lower status than the jobs they had left behind them in the West Indies' (Dalphinis 1991: 46). We can assume that most of the migrants were not in fact speakers of the basilect alone, but commanded a range of styles somewhere in the middle of the continuum. Furthermore, most migrants defined *themselves* as English speakers:

> it must be said that Jamaicans consider themselves speakers of English, and are offended when ignorant English people inquire what their mother tongue might be. When they come to live and work in England they expect no language difficulties such as they know would await them in, say, Panama or Cuba. Jamaicans usually claim to be able to understand everything said in Standard English; it comes as something of a shock to many of them to find that English people can by no means always understand them. (J.C. Wells, 1973: 3)

This was certainly the case with Mrs S., the mother of one of my teenage informants, born in rural Jamaica about 1930, who moved to London about 1960:

> I've never work – I've never really work when I was back in de West Indies my husband work, I worked when I came over here and I [took a long time] to get a job – because I could remember work at de Post Office and I when I pronounce my words you know too [soft] dey say dey don't hunderstand – according to dem dey don't hunderstand me, my haccent maybe it's my haccent or what dey don' understan' it or ting an' I feel like I'm speakin' the same English like over here.

Mrs S., though her speech shows some grammatical influences from Creole and a strong Jamaican accent, certainly was not speaking Jamaican Creole on this occasion. This does not, mean, of course, that she *cannot* speak Jamaican Creole, just that to characterise the whole of her generation as 'Creole speakers' is much too simple. At the time of the recording, Mrs S. had lived in Britain nearly twenty-five years. Her speech will almost certainly have adapted in some respects towards the London English of her neighbours – this is the process documented (for accent) by J.C. Wells in *Jamaican Pronunciation in London* (1973). It is difficult to say what her speech would have been like in 1960 when she first arrived in London. But Wright (1984) stresses that 'even the most acrolectal speaker' in Jamaica has a passive knowledge of Creole: in Jamaica 'JC is a stylistic option, primarily for informal situations' (Wright 1984: 33).

A second problem with the 'diglossia' paradigm is that 'Creole' has distinct meanings for the different generations. For the first generation, 'Creole' will be the vernacular of a particular territory: for example, Jamaica, Guyana, Trinidad, Barbados. In some cases it will mean the French-based Creole of Dominica or St Lucia. However, for the second generation, as we have seen, 'Creole' or 'Patois' is focused specifically on *Jamaican* Creole. In many cases this is quite unlike the vernacular of the parents' country or countries. It would not even be appropriate for the child to speak to the parent in this Creole if the parent is not from Jamaica.

A third problem with the 'diglossia' approach is the notion that different languages are used mainly or exclusively in different domains. Of this view of bilingualism, Martin-Jones (1991: 50) writes: 'As the empirical work in bilingual communities has developed, it has become clear that the languages within the communicative repertoire of bilingual minority groups do not necessarily fall into a neat pattern of complementary distribution across domains.' One difficulty is that whereas in London, London English is felt to be appropriate in nearly all situations, Creole is appropriate only in some of these. Even in the situations where it is appropriate, Creole will only be used some of the time – in fact, a very small proportion of the time, if my informants and their families are typical. Generally it is true to say that use of Creole is restricted to the private domain, and informal situations. Even in these situations, however, first generation Caribbeans are more likely to use a variety close to the local Standard English of their birthplace than the Creole, while the second generation are much more likely to use London English than a form of Creole. Furthermore, when Creole is used by the younger generation, it is almost always used *in conjunction with* London English in a code switching mode. This fact is strikingly obvious to a linguist listening carefully to a conversation, but is not part of the 'folk linguistics' of the community itself, who usually talk in terms of either speaking 'ordinary English' or 'chattin' Patois'. Although individuals may be aware of sometimes talking in 'a mixture' this is very rarely commented on. It is therefore not accessible to research by questioning community members. The only way to study it is to analyse actual conversational interactions.

Attitudes and Uses

It follows from the last paragraph that there are at least two different ways of studying a community's use of language and attitudes towards it. One way is to ask members of that community about their language use and the usage of others in the community, as they perceive it. The result will be a collection of information about that community's *overt* language attitudes: how they feel they *should*, or others *do*, behave.

A second approach is to make a detailed study of people's language *practices*. This presents more difficulties for the researcher, who has to do a great deal of interpretation in order to make inferences from what people *actually* do to their *motivations* for doing it.

These approaches can complement each other. Although people do not always do what they say they do, where there is a mismatch between what they do and say, we can assume that there is some reason for this. Inferences based on the differences between self-reported and observed behaviour have become standard methodology in sociolinguistics since the work of Labov. Usually such inferences have been based on quantitative analyses of single variables – nearly always phonological variables, such as the incidence of postvocalic /r/ in New York speech (Labov 1966). In this study I have not attempted such quantitative analyses, but I still believe that good use can be made of a combination of the two approaches. In the remainder of this chapter I will report some of the attitudes and beliefs about language expressed by some of my young informants. I will then go on to present some examples of language in use in conversation, to show how these attitudes relate to actual practice.

Creole and English in the home

Some Caribbean parents are known to disapprove of their children using Creole. This may reflect the generally negative view of Creole in the West Indies, especially within the education system, coupled with the view that British English is necessary for children to 'get on' in Britain in education and in life generally. Dalphinis (1991: 9) notes:

> Creole is spoken by the older generation, among themselves and is also used to the younger generation. However, there is an expectation that children should use English and not Patwa to their parents. This non-reciprocal pattern of usage is closely linked with expectations that the younger person should not be held back as they make their way through an English-speaking educational system by an over-familiarity with Patwa.

Several informants in my study articulated the view that their parents *preferred* them to speak British English:

> Mom – mom likes me to speak mostly English, she said when I go out into, you know, upper class society, and I start speakin' Patois dey might not understand, and take me as an idiot. She just want me to get used to de plain English first. So when I go out to Jamaicans or West Indians, like I just talk my native tongue. (Steve, fifteen. Jamaican parents)

> A   Your parents don't really like you speakin' bad.

> MS   *Do they get very upset if you talk Patois?*

> A   Yeh, my mum does. (Annie, 17, mother from St Vincent, father from Trinidad)

> They [parents] feel . . . I should save that type of language for when I go back to the West Indies. (Stephen, fifteen. Barbadian parents)

Not all adolescents agree with this view, however. This is shown in the following discussion between two boys aged fifteen from South East London, Shane (Barbadian father, American mother) and Chris (both parents Jamaican). In the course of defending Creole against Shane's objections, Chris actually begins to *use* Creole, distancing his own talk from that of Shane and putting into practice his own belief that 'if you want them to know your culture you have to chat it'. (Underlined stretches of talk in the following are those which are identifiably 'Creole' in phonology or grammar.)

S   So I would say, right, to chat Patois, right, I mean it's sometimes – it shows the people that you're lacking intelligence. If you look at it in a certain way, right, it shows your ignorance, I mean you're over in England, right, for so long – I mean to say you should know what to chat in front of certain people, right? So I would say to chat Patois, you know, as a t'ing, you know, it's a bit silly to me – at home, yes, in your own environment, but when you're around white people chatting Patois, to me it looks tedious.

C   It might seem tedious to you, but it might be interesting to them – because I mean to say, if you <u>waant</u> them to know your <u>culture you afi chat it</u> [*afi* = 'have to']

S   So what you're saying there is that if you're to show your culture you have to chat Patois.

<u>Well if you want if you want exchange it den well you afi chat it.</u>

S   I think you're talking shite you know mate.

C   I'm <u>talkin' what I t'ink</u>

One boy said he could not help using Creole even though he thought it might be bad for him:

MS   *Do you agree with your mother that speaking Patois can hold you back?*
S   Yeah, it could but – sometimes you don't – it's like talking normal you don't you can't even, you don't even know what you're talkin' sometimes. When you actually stop and fink about what you just said, you say oh no, I slipped back into Patois. <u>T'ing</u> like that. (Stephen, fifteen. Barbadian parents)

In some families parents react negatively if children use Creole when talking to them:

You talk like that most to your friends but. You wouldn't really sort of come out with things like that to your parents . . . you sort of do it less. (Barry, seventeen. Jamaican parents)

However, several informants indicated that parents have a

more relaxed attitude to their children using Creole when they are somewhat older. For example:

> You see like, the parents who come over from the West Indies, they try and teach their children this attitude 'you're English, you was born here, so you must talk the right and proper way, so you mustn't talk like that', but then after a time, as you get older, they don't really worry about it too much. (Barry, seventeen. Jamaican parents)

> MS: *Will your parents disapprove if you use it?*

> No not really – they just sit down and they listen to me and they'll say something – 'Brenda where you come from?' [laughs] somefin' like that , you know what I mean, cause I'm born English so they aks me what I want to speak Patois for? As if I'm from Jamaica or whatever. (Brenda, seventeen. Jamaican parents)

Many black adolescents I talked to were conscious of the differences between their own Creole and their parents'. One younger girl (herself an accomplished user of *Jamaican* Creole) found her mother's Barbadian a source of amusement:

> Right, my mum right, when she goes – like some English people go 'can you go and get me a glass of water please' mum go – 'get me a piece o' waata please' – not [wɔːtə], '[waːta]' an' 'piece'. You don't get water in pieces do you? She goes 'get me a piece of waata' like that – but she jus' makes me laugh . . . an' she speaks so fas' she comes from Barbados she's Barbadian, my dad's Trinidadian. (Cheryl, twelve)

This was echoed by another boy:

> You see, my mom right, she says some words to me, right, sometimes, right, wha' I can't understand you know an' I sort of start laughin', but then again right, y' know, I can understand some o' de words which she says to me y' know – I even speak it back to her, y' see. (Vincent, fifteen. Jamaican parents)

Some adolescents seemed concerned about a lack of knowledge or deficiency in Creole on their own part:

For my English oral, last year, I had to read a Patois poem, so I aksed my mum to read it for me, and that's how I got to, you know, sort of pick it up just for that poem . . . kept letting her read it over and over again till I get the sound. Then I read it, in my English oral . . . I'm not as good, [as her], no. My [older] sisters can't even speak it. (Brenda, seventeen. Jamaican parents)

This speaker and others commented on the differences in the Jamaican and British types of Creole:

The sound, the way [they speak] – it's more or less the same, it is the same, same words the same everyfing, but – the way my parents speak it, it doesn't sound affected, put it that way, it's more like me and you speaking now, it's more fluent, and not so harsh – but when we speak it's sort of h-heavy tongue, I dunno. (Brenda, seventeen. Jamaican parents)

I mean, what I'm saying is that I've come across many of dem who try to speak the Jamaican language, er, the Jamaican Patois, but how they speak it is totally different, becau' they've got the English accent, and um, dey, becau' they've got the English accent they try to speak the Jamaican local Patois the same way and in doin' so it sounds really terrible you know it sort of sounds you know it's really funny. (Errol, twenty, born in England, lived age four to eighteen in Jamaica)

Brenda (seventeen, Jamaican parents) commented that in Jamaica she had been teased as a 'foreigner' because her Creole was not up to scratch:

Oh, they call you all – 'English gyal, come here English gyal!' yeh, my sister 'ad it all, my sister ain't English, my sister's Jamaican, because she come over here when she was young, when she went back over there they were callin' her English gyal, the *lot* [lɑt] but when she, she ain't forget nothin', she can still speak it so she open her mouth and they say *sorry* [sɑri]! Then they pick on my cousin.

By simply questioning informants it is difficult to get an accurate picture of where and when Creole is actually used at home. Answers tend to be vague and general, and sometimes phrased in terms of domains or interlocutors, as in the following description:

Well they don't really use it, like, well, now and then, like if we're all in the family, if like my mum's going to say somefing, right, she won't say 'Wayne would you go do de dishes please', she'll say [wiɛn gɒ dʊ) di dɪʃɪz] somep'n like dat – she would say it in a West Indian talk but normally if like if there's a visitor or something it would be plain English . . . It's like slang like, if two people don't know each other they talk like formally but if two people know each uvver they use slang, you know to get across because they know each other personally. (Wayne, seventeen, Guyanese parents)

However, there is general agreement that using Creole is more appropriate with 'friends' than with members of the older generation.

MS *When do you feel you would use Patois and when would you talk as you're talking to me now?*

B When I'm amongst my friends – messin' about, you know, joke about an' have a laugh then you hear all of it come out. That's when I'm at work or at home – sometimes I use it at home, not often. (Brenda, seventeen, Jamaican parents)

If we put these fragments of information together, we can construct a picture of black adolescents' *perceptions* of Creole use and attitudes which is similar to that given by Sutcliffe. Creole is used variably by the parents' generation, but not usually when persons from outside are present. Some parents are wholly negative towards their children's use of Creole, but some are mainly concerned that *young* children should not use Creole, and are more relaxed about teenagers speaking it. Among adolescents, there is a feeling that Creole is appropriate 'among friends' of the same generation, but not for use with parents, except in a few circumstances. British-born teenagers have some insecurities about their own abilities in speaking Creole.

Conversations in the Family

In this section I will use a study of conversations within Caribbean families to try to put more detail on the pattern of language use which has emerged from community members' own reports. I will rely mainly on conversations which were recorded in family homes by members of the families who lived there. It is not possible to say that these families were typical of *all* Caribbean families in London. However, it would be surprising if their behaviour were completely atypical. In this discussion I will refer mainly to extracts from the conversations reproduced in Appendix 2 of this book. Although for reasons of space only parts of the conversations have been transcribed and reproduced here, for several of the conversations the extracts are just long enough to give a flavour of the content and tone of the conversation in general. I recommend the reader to read through the conversations in Appendix 2 to get a general impression of them before returning to this chapter and the next to read the discussion of detailed points.

Styles and switches

London Caribbean households typically are home to speakers of several different language varieties. While the younger generation will all know and use London English and the older generation will have knowledge of a Creole variety, the actual patterns of use involve a complex interplay between these varieties and others. We have already seen how in the Caribbean, a continuum of dialects is the norm. Different individuals may place themselves at different points in the middle of the continuum and use a range of varieties above and below their 'home base'. The same is true for those Caribbeans who have moved to London, with the additional complication that they will accommodate to a greater or lesser extent to the norms of London English, as shown by J.C. Wells (1973). For at least some people of the first generation, Creole has symbolic value as a language of black identity, and those individuals may try to maintain their 'Caribbeanness' by keeping their speech as close to Creole as possible. This is especially true of Rastafarians, for whom language has special symbolic importance (see Chapter 1). Other individuals may assimilate more readily to London English speech. Ultimately the degree of assimilation may depend on the amount of contact with native speakers of London English – including members of the speaker's own family.

British-born speakers, on the other hand, occupy a position which allows them to mediate both linguistically and culturally between the Caribbean and Britain. As native speakers of London English *and* having a knowledge of Creole, they have 'a foot in each camp'. To a greater extent than other members of the community they can use both of these languages or 'codes', wielding their respective symbolic values *strategically* within conversation. This gives rise to the code-switching behaviour in conversation with other black people which is characteristic of British-born black speakers.

It is striking that in London Caribbean families where there are several individuals each with their own characteristic style of talk (for example, the S. family of Conversation A) there seems to be little pressure to conform to a single 'family norm'. Widely differing accents and a range of grammatical forms from near-basilectal Creole to British Standard can be heard from different individuals participating in a single conversation. Given the common Caribbean background of family members it is noteworthy that Creole is *not* used as a common medium of interaction either within or between generations, at least when British-born speakers are present; however, some speakers may use a mesolectal Creole most of the time without it apparently having or acquiring any special symbolic value. At the same time, British-born speakers will use Creole rarely, and when they do, it is not primarily to accommodate to other speakers using Creole, as we shall see. Listening to many of the conversations which make up my data, one has the impression that they take place in a climate of 'linguistic tolerance', where many different degrees of 'Creoleness' and 'Englishness' are accepted. Against this background, the British-born speakers show especially differentiated behaviour, sticking mostly to London English but occasionally manifesting strategic switches into Creole.

Inter-generational talk

In conversations which involve speakers of both the first and second generations it is mainly the behaviour of the second generation speakers which is of interest, for it is these individuals who have 'stylistic mobility' between London English and Creole and can be assumed to be using the two codes differentially (though not necessarily consciously) in a strategic way. The question we need to ask and answer, then, is whether second generation speakers consistently display differential behaviour dependent on the generation of their interlocutors.

One pattern of language use which has been observed in some bilingual communities is that of reciprocal language use. If A addresses B in language L, then B's response to A will be in L as well. It is easy to see how such behaviour could originate out of necessity (if B is bilingual, but A monolingual in L) and be extended even to cases where both speakers are bilingual, out of a need to show solidarity or to conform to norms of politeness within the community.

In Conversation A, the British-born speaker Brenda uses both London English and Creole, but shows what seems to be differential behaviour in responding towards her father (F) and her brother (L), for example, in A–3:

Extract 1: Conversation A–3

```
        L    society don't like dem t'ings dere in first place, right, (0.4)
             you know wha' I mean, dem hafi be lock (0.8) (up)
   5    B    m::
        L  ⎡ because society (don't want them in it)
 →      B  ⎣ because, because them start / it off in first place dey know
             it's wrong (.)
```

Brenda's brother (L) is Jamaican-born and has a strong Caribbean accent. His turn here is also marked by Creole grammatical features like *hafi* ('have to'). Brenda's response begins in overlap with the end of his turn, and begins in Creole, switching to London English only at the end. Brenda here appears to be accommodating to her brother by using Creole. However, only seconds later, Brenda overlaps with her father (who also uses Caribbean-accented English, though with more Standard syntax than L), but this time in London English:

Extract 2: Conversation A–3

```
        ?    right dem (no really)
  10    B    so dey know 'ow to (1.0) put ⎡ a stop to it
        F                                 ⎣ yeh but I say what I'm saying,
             it shouldn't be so ⎡ that's what I'm saying, it shouldn't be so
 →      B                       ⎣ it shouldn't be so, but it is so
```

In this case, Brenda not only accommodates to her father's language variety (Standard English, in terms of syntax) but actually echoes his words in agreement in the first part of her turn.

Reciprocal use of Creole or English is not the norm in the community under study, however. British-born speakers tend to use London English most of the time anyway, and there appears to be no requirement to use Creole to respond to Creole utterances, at least from adults:

Extract 3: Conversation E–3

```
1   V   where's the knife mum?
    (2.4)
    M   Lord (munumun) look fe someting man! Cha (1.0)
        where's a dis where's a that (1.2) find it unu self man
5   V   ih hi hi hi
    (1.2)
    M   uh huh
    V   all right, there's no need to shout
```

It is certainly the case that British-born Caribbeans *do* use Creole from time to time in the presence of their Caribbean-born elders. However, it would be wrong to think that they use Creole mainly in response to Creole utterances. Rather, they use Creole as part of their overall language-mixing strategy, invoking the Creole/English dichotomy for its symbolic value in similar ways, whether speaking to their own generation or an older one. For example, earlier in Conversation E, there is a rare exchange in Creole between Laverne and her aunt (M):

Extract 4: Conversation E–2

```
1    M   Laverne a your turn to wash up the dishes
→    L   I said me na a do it <giggle>
     M   you a joke man/ (0.8) come on man (you no) / finish wi'
         what you doin' (there) an wash the dishes come on man
5   (L)  <laughs> Na(hh)aew
```

Here M's indirect request for L to wash the dishes is in Caribbean accented English with a Creole grammatical structure (*a* for Standard *it is*.) Laverne's refusal is also unambiguously in Creole. However, this itself does not indicate a 'reciprocal' use of Creole, for similar refusals can occur elsewhere in response to requests *not* in Creole:

Extract 5: (Recorded by the informant, Errol, and two male friends.)

1	E	'ey, did you go out yet
	P	(oh) let me ge% a drink
	W	yeah, dis mornin'
	?D	ge% me some wa – get me / (one)
5	P	<u>na:, me na ge% not'in' f' you</u>
	L	get me a drink Patrick
→	P	<u>no% (.) a ge% no%in' f' you (0.8) 'cause</u>
	?	a ha ha ha
	W	this mornin'

In ordinary conversation, disagreements and refusals are usually interpretable as face-threatening. They show disapproval of the addressee's views and may make the addressee feel bad about him/herself. Agreements, on the other hand, offer support and endorsement of the addressee's view and are likely to make him/her feel good. In many cultures this leads to an asymmetry between ways of offering agreements and disagreements in talk: agreements are given more immediately, are more frequent, and are given openly, while disagreements are relatively infrequent and are hedged about with hesitations and excuses: see Pomerantz (1984) for an extended discussion.

What is striking about the refusals in the two extracts above is that both are given immediately, without any pause, and both are met with following laughter. Thus this potentially serious and face-threatening act – of refusing a polite request, immediately and without excuse – is treated by both the requester and the refuser as non-serious, eliciting laughter.

By contrast, Laverne's refusal of the same request earlier in E–1, this time in London English, is marked as 'joking' by *preceding laughter* from the speaker herself.

Extract 6: Conversation E–1

	M	<u>unu better go wash up di dishes!</u>
	L	eh heh he he no: I was gonna take he he I'm gonna take, um Natasha over the park / there
10	M	o:h!

This refusal is much more of a 'classic' polite refusal: it is not immediate (being offset instead by laughter, which also marks it as 'non-serious') and is immediately followed by an excuse ('I'm gonna take Natasha over the park'), which could also be seen as a bid to be treated as doing something equivalently onerous: looking after a child instead of washing up.

In the context of Conversation E, then, using Creole to express a refusal marks it as 'jocular' and non-threatening, just as laughter, delay and offering an excuse (or 'alternative') were used earlier to mark another refusal as non-threatening. I will discuss the 'joking' uses of Creole in more detail later. The point of these examples is that using Creole to refuse a request is a way of building a particular meaning into the refusal. The use of Creole need not be a response to a prior use of Creole.

Conversation A 'Is society right?' has the special characteristic of being a rather abstract discussion (unlike Conversation E, which deals with the most stereotypically mundane of domestic topics!). In this conversation several first generation speakers are present, and both British English and Creole are used at different times. In a discussion of this nature, much of the talk is part of the argument, propositions offered for comment and evaluation to the group as a whole. Other parts of the talk relate to the management of the conversation itself.

Participants in the conversation show an awareness of the difference between these two types of talk. Talk which forms part of the *argument* normally expects and receives evaluations from other participants. The preferred response – the most likely one – is agreement, shown by the use of agreement tokens like 'yeah', 'right', repetition of the last speaker's key words, etc., as in Extract 7 below.

Extract 7: Conversation A–1

```
        B                                           if there wasn't no
 →              halfcastes then you could distinguish, right
10  ?F   distinguish
```

Less frequently an utterance may meet with disagreement from the other parties to the conversation. For example, in A–1, lines 1–3, Brenda makes a statement and her father disagrees:

Extract 8: Conversation A–1

```
1→ B   it's only because there's halfcastes in it now, right
       ┌ why (0.4) there's a mixup
   F   └ no no no, I'm not talkin' I'm not ┌ sayin'
   L                                        └ no no
```

In everyday conversation where participants direct their utterances toward one another, such disagreements are usually face-
threatening and are avoided.[1] This is especially true of very
strong disagreements like Brenda's father's disagreement in Extract 8, with his 'no' repeated three times in overlap with Brenda's talk, and his continuing to talk over her with repeated uses
of 'not'. In the context of the discussion, however, this disagreement is not treated as face-threatening: it is not directed at Brenda's personal position but at a proposition (that the existence of
'halfcastes' has confused racial boundaries) which she has articulated and which is now 'up for grabs'. Thus a disagreement
which would be face-threatening – and therefore avoided – in
'ordinary' conversation is permissible, and non-threatening, within the confines of the discussion.

Thus within this conversation, we can say that there are actually two types of talk (at least) going on: *argument*, where
some of the rules of politeness governing conversation are tempo-
rarily suspended, and *management*, where they continue to hold.
British-born speakers respond to the difference between these by
showing differential language behaviour in the two types of talk.
For example, in Extract 9, Brenda's frustrated 'daddy PLEASE' is
an attempt at managing the conversation directed specifically towards her father, and is in London English.

Extract 9: Conversation A–2

```
    B   I always say, right
 5  L   * * that's it, that's it
    B   I always say, right,
   (0.4)
    F   and he know he can't finish it too
 → B   daddy PLEASE!
10  ?   (yeh) he know ┌ too
 → B                  └ I always say, right, if at first you poor [pʊəɹ],
        right, an' den you get rich, when you lose it all you no feel
        no way cause you know you can still ru:n
```

However, Brenda's contribution to the *argument* at lines 11–13 – which she has signalled several times with Standard 'I always say, right' – involves a switch from London English to Creole. The key part of her proposition, furthermore, is the Creole part. Similarly in (10) when she addresses her father *directly* she does this in London English.

Extract 10: Conversation A–1

```
        ?L   (cause) I ⎡ know * true
        F              ⎣ no sir no sir
   20→B        yes daddy, oh come off it, there's (Holly)
        R      * generation * it's a whole generation
               you no ⎡ see it
        F              ⎣ (yes a can't be full black)
        L      it's a way it's a way ⎡ (0.4) how do you t'ink seh,
   25→B                               ⎣ whe you mean?
        L      how do you know what you is, dat's what me
```

while *whe you mean* at line 25 overlaps with the turn of her brother L, to whom it is addressed. Key phrases used by Brenda in this part of the conversation, meanwhile, are in Creole: 'im stone black and halfcastes, both used several times.

In this conversation then, we can see two patterns. In talk directed towards *specific* participants, such as Brenda's father and her brother, Brenda tends to accommodate to the addressee's preferred variety. In her brother's case this is Creole, but in her father's case, London English. This reflects the pattern of generation-oriented use which speakers themselves reported: Creole only (but not exclusively) with peers, 'ordinary' English with parents and their generation. However, talk within the argument and not addressed to a specified individual may be in Creole or in British English, with a single turn often containing elements of both.

Conversation E on the other hand, shows us that there are 'licensed' uses of Creole by second-generation speakers even with their parents' generation. However, such use is always motivated and when it occurs, Creole carries a symbolic value which it imparts to the utterance in question. For example, in E–2 (Extracts 4 and 6), the use of Creole puts a gloss 'jocular' on the utterance in which it occurs. The effect is to mitigate the speaker's refusal of a reasonable request.

Talk with small children

There are few examples in my data of interactions with small children. The clearest is from conversation D–6, where Valerie talks to the baby in both English and Creole:

Extract 11: Conversation D–6

	V	blow the bubbles Courtney
20	ba	a:: nye
	V	Courtney, blow the bubbles
	(5.0)	
23	V	Courtney, look how ya aunty do ya hair and look how it stay now!=
	=	<laughter (1.5)>
25	V	watch a 'souly' look now, alright!

Superficially, lines 19, 21, 23, and (perhaps) 25 are all addressed to 'Courtney', who is addressed by name in each of these. However, if we look at Valerie's behaviour just before this in the conversation, it is apparent that actually not all this talk is intended for the baby.

Extract 12: Conversation D–6

	C	dribble dribble (4.0) dribble dribble
15		
	(2.0)	
	V	(you see him play wid) di bubble ⌈ dem!
		⌊ <laughter (2.0)>
	(3.0)	
	V	blow the bubbles Courtney

Line 17 is clearly *not* addressed to the baby, but to the two other women present. It echoes Colette's 'She's trying to blow a bubble here *me no know*'. Their response is laughter – the same as their response to line 23, which ostensibly *is* addressed to 'Courtney'. It seems likely that the utterances which are 'really' intended for Courtney are those short London English sentences: 'Shut up Courtney' at line 29 of D–1, 'Say Andrea' several times in D–6, and 'Courtney, blow the bubbles'. (See Appendix 2 for the complete extract.)

In this case, it seems that Creole is being used, perhaps with its 'jocular' symbolic value, to *comment* on the baby and its 'cute' activities. Line 23 of Extract 11, though ostensibly intended for 'Courtney' is actually for the benefit of the other women, and elicits the desired response – laughter – from them. Line 25 is probably of the same type.

This is only one example, and it is not possible to generalise from this to comment on language behaviour towards Caribbean babies in general. However, we can see here an example of how children may be exposed at a very early age to purposeful code-switching behaviour.

Intra-generational talk among young black Londoners

It should by now be clear that the language behaviour of young black Londoners of Caribbean background can only be described with reference to patterns of code-switching, between the two perceived varieties 'ordinary English' (which in practice means London English) and 'Patois', which I have argued is a variety of Jamaican Creole.

In the discussion of inter-generational talk it emerged that code switching from English to Creole was relatively infrequent, and was not usually as a response to another speaker using Creole, although it sometimes was. Code switching in intra-generational talk is such a complex matter that it merits a chapter to itself, and the whole of the next chapter is devoted to it. In this section I want to deal only with the question of *selection* of a code for a particular interaction.

The diglossic approach to bilingualism would have us look for particular domains where Creole might be selected in preference to British English for interactions among second- generation speakers. More precisely, we might look for a set of conditions or circumstances which lead to the expectation that Creole would be used in an interaction. Sutcliffe, for example, (1982a: 148) indicates that his informants reported that they used 'Jamaican Creole' with black interlocutors in the playground. It is very important, though, to understand exactly what this means. The social act of 'chattin' Patois' is *not* the same as the linguistic act of 'speaking Creole'. If speakers report using Creole or 'Patois' in a specified situation, this means that the use of Creole is *licensed* for that situation. It may *actually* be used little or not at all in a particular interaction.

Thus while from the point of view of community members, situations may fall into the categories of 'Patois' (e.g. playground interactions with other black children) or 'non-Patois' (e.g. talking to a teacher), what this means is that in a 'Patois' situation, it is permitted to use Creole at certain times. In a 'non-Patois' situation, no use of Creole would normally be appropriate. In a 'Patois' situation, each participant may choose to use Creole or not, and to an extent to which that speaker feels comfortable. Thus even in a situation where Creole is permitted, none may in fact be spoken – or if it is, it may be limited to ritualised tokens such as the tags *man*, *guy* and *star*, which, though they lie within the boundaries of the folk concept 'Patois' are best seen as part of the language of black-influenced youth culture.

In practice, the amount of Creole used in any interaction is the subject of ongoing negotiation among the parties themselves. We saw that in inter-generational talk, responding to utterances in Creole was *not* a primary motivation for a speaker to switch to Creole. It is true for intra-generational talk as well that speakers are not constrained to use Creole to respond to a Creole utterance. In fact, if we look at a conversation like Conversation B or Conversation D, where all the participants are British-born and in their late teens or twenties, it is most often the case that a Creole utterance does *not* receive a Creole response. Creole utterances in conversations like these are usually one-liners. The following extracts are typical.

Extract 13: Conversation B–4

```
     B    'e was going to build 'is place (0.6)
         ⌈ 'im a build 'is business (1.0)
 10  ?   ⌊ ye:h e was NI:CE man
```

Extract 14: Conversation D–1

```
 45  L    hih that's me! (0.6) ⌈ Valerie cut me off there bwo::y!
     C                         ⌊ (must be the one in my bathroom)
     V    no I never! It's just my wardrobe that's all
```

However, there are certainly interactions which involve the use of more Creole than this. The question then arises as to what promotes a greater use of Creole in conversation. The single most important factor seems to be a preference on the part of *all* parties present for using Creole. Since this is one aspect of the 'ongoing negotiation' and preferences of 'newcomers' to the interaction cannot be assumed at the outset, the circumstances which will most favour a speedy agreement to use Creole are those where there are few participants – ideally the minimum, two – and these individuals are already well known to each other, and known to favour Creole. Thus the stereotype which exists within the community itself, of two close friends gossiping in Patois, corresponds to reality – with the proviso that even in such conversations, code switching between Creole and British English will take place. In extract 15, for example, Cheryl's Creole response is to the London English part of Jane's turn, while Jane's next turn is an English response to Cheryl's Creole turn.

Extract 15: Conversation G

```
1    J    * * * she never did invite me (0.2) are YOU goin'
     C    no she never invite me neither
     J    's not fair
```

We saw in Chapter 2 part of the process of 'negotiating Creole' in a conversation between two British-born girls, one of whom used Creole extensively, the other only rarely and tokenistically. A preference for using Creole is certainly related to individual cultural values, as Edwards and Sutcliffe found in their West Midlands study. An important factor is the birthplace of the interlocutors. Even Caribbeans under the age of twenty may have been born outside Britain, and there is a wide range of degrees of exposure to Caribbean language and culture, so conversations even among age-mates may nevertheless incorporate a mixture of Caribbean-born and British-born participants. Where there are several Caribbean-born individuals, or others like Rastafarians who put especially high value on the use of Creole, then Creole may be the language of preference for the whole conversation. Even so, code switching in such conversations is the norm for British-born speakers in my sample.

For example, in Conversation C, the players in the domino game are mostly male and Jamaican-born. There are no 'outsiders' or older Caribbeans, so the conditions favour maximum use of Creole. The 'language of the game' is thus Creole or strongly Creole-influenced English. Even so, London English is used as well, for example by the British-born Brenda at line 6, responding to M's London-accented Creole turn at line 1:

Extract 16: Conversation C–3

```
 1   M    you wan% a swee%ie?
     (2.8)
     N    you got ONE?
     M    m:hm (.) one that (you suck)
 5   (5.0)
     B    can I have sixty please?
     M    me na sell sweet now y'know (0.5) you want buy quar%ers
     N    hahaha (.) blodklaat! ⌈ if you give 'em free Brenda wouldn't
     B                          ⌊ him want one (for eat)
10   M    want it hahaha
```

Meanwhile the speaker N uses a Creole obscenity in line 8, but goes on to make an ironic comment on Brenda's request in London English; but this overlaps with Brenda's next turn, which this time is an ironic comment on N's behaviour, and is in Creole.

What this shows is that there is no simple relationship between domains, situations, generations or language preferences which will enable us to explain the linguistic behaviour of young British-born Caribbeans in London. The best we can do is to make a close study of code switching and hope that it will provide an overall framework for understanding how the two perceived varieties, Creole and English, interact in conversation. This is the subject of the next chapter.

Note

1   This has been demonstrated (cf. Pomerantz 1975, 1984) to hold true for interactions among *middle-class* speakers of English in some communities. It is not certain, however, that it is universal; different communities certainly have different notions of what constitutes a 'face-threatening act'. Therefore, the claims made here should be taken with this caveat.

7 Code Switching in Conversation

It is probably true to say that if young British-born Caribbeans from London have a conversation lasting longer than a few turns, then it will contain London English even if it contains Creole as well. Thus the interaction between Creole and English in the talk of this group is of central interest to anyone studying the linguistic behaviour of black Londoners. The principal means whereby the two language varieties interact in conversation is through language alternation in the form of code switching.

Over the last two decades the study of code switching has attracted a great deal of interest from researchers working in different areas of linguistics. Because of the fact that code switching, when it occurs, is pervasive in bilinguals' speech, and defies analysis on any one level, individual researchers have tended to focus on just those few aspects of code switching which are of particular relevance to them. Hence particular research programmes have generally centred on one of three broad areas of code-switching phenomena:

(1) The formal aspects of code switching, in particular the grammatical mechanisms whereby a bilingual individual can produce a sentence (or sentence-like utterance) partly in one language and partly in another, where the respective parts still apparently conform to the rules of the language they are expressed in.

(2) Pragmatic and discoursal aspects of code switching – what factors within a particular encounter motivate speakers to switch and what meanings underlie speakers' switches. Re-

searchers with this focus typically are concerned to provide a typology or taxonomy of switches which relates tokens (i.e. individual switches) to types. They may also be concerned with relating these types to the symbolic meaning of each code within the community (an aim which brings them within the scope of (3) below) and even seek to establish a theory with predictive power, i.e. the ability to predict instances of switching within a stretch of discourse.

(3) Ethnographic description of code switching – called by Auer (1984a: 96) the 'macro-sociological approach, usually associated with the question "who speaks what language to whom and when" (Fishman 1965)'. This '4W' approach, according to Auer 'takes the unproblematic existence and relevance of patterns of language choice for granted'. Researchers in this tradition have focused on questions of the status of switching within a community, its relation to other phenomena such as language maintenance (e.g. the survival of a language among a migrant community in their new home) or language death (the decline and demise of such a language).

Most researchers focus on just one of these aspects, although some, such as Gumperz, Poplack and Myers-Scotton, combine (1), (2) and (3) to varying extents. The formal aspects of code switching (1) are most likely to be studied in isolation from the others. Clearly (2) and (3) are related, as an understanding of community norms and attitudes to bilingual behaviour is necessary to an account of the pragmatics of switching, and perhaps vice versa. It is less immediately evident that such an understanding should be necessary in order to account for the formal properties of code switching, although I would argue strongly that it is, inasmuch as the extent to which switching may take place is in part a function of the extent to which the codes involved have 'fused' within a community, i.e. how interchangeable they are for the different purposes of everyday interaction.

In focusing on different and only partly overlapping areas for research in code switching, researchers differentiate themselves as sharply by their methodology as by their interests. Formal studies of code switching thus tend to deal with idealised or edited data, to which syntactic theories are applied: e.g. Phrase Structure Grammar (Joshi 1985); Government and Binding (Di Sciullo et al. 1986); Lexical-Functional Grammar (Myers-Scotton 1992). Research in the pragmatic-discoursal and macro-sociological traditions, on the other hand, almost always uses transcribed conversational data, though in a variety of different ways. For example, the conversation analytic (CA) approach requires a minutely detailed transcription in order to focus on sequential features of the conversation, while the more macro-sociological approach of Gumperz uses less detailed transcriptions and places as much emphasis on participants' *post hoc* explanations of the code switching as on a detailed display of the continuing talk.

Codes compared

A majority of studies of code switching have studied pairs of languages which are very different from one another in terms of structure and vocabulary: for example, Spanish and English (Poplack 1980). A smaller number of studies have dealt with closely related dialects or languages, for example, Blom and Gumperz's 1972 study of code-switching between 'official' and 'local' varieties of Norwegian in a small town. Although there are many points of divergence between 'Creole' and 'English', there are also sufficient similarities for many people, linguists and native speakers among them, to refer to Creole as a variety of English. The present study therefore falls into the less well-researched area of code switching between closely related varieties, and there are some special problems associated with this.

For research focused on *formal* aspects of code switching, much of the interest lies in the process whereby two widely divergent grammatical systems are made compatible in such a way that switching is possible between them: hence researchers in this area have mainly concentrated on pairs of languages that have no more than chance (or universal) similarities. In the case of the more pragmatically orientated studies, there are other reasons why linguists have preferred to study languages which are very different from each other. In order to have a sense of how the different codes are used in interactions, it is necessary for the linguist to be quite clear about which code is being used at a particular time. For a researcher who is not a member of the community under study – which is nearly always the case – it may be difficult to decide which utterances belong to which code, in the case where the two languages in contact are very similar. This is well demonstrated by Gumperz (1982: 85) in discussing an earlier study of Hindi and Punjabi used by college students in Delhi (Gumperz 1971): 'The two codes here appear indistinguishable phonetically and almost identical in both syntax and lexicon. To juxtapose such sequences in natural conversational contexts, participants must be sensitive to what to the outsider may appear as quite subtle perceptual cues.'

This is a serious problem for the 'outsider' linguist, who may not be able to trust his/her intuition to decide which code is in use at a particular time. The alternative – to ask a native informant for judgements – is also fraught with problems in this case. Linguists are not agreed on the desirability of using native speaker judgements in code-switching research; cf. Auer's remark that 'It seems to be a rash conclusion to prefer informants' comments on co-participants' behaviour to the analyst's reconstructive work' (Auer 1984b: 94) and Gumperz' view that 'I think generally speaking we cannot but use informants' reports' (1971: 112).

Although code switching is as much an 'insider' activity as talking itself for those communities which practise it, it is remarkable that most communities do not have a set of 'folk linguistic' categories which relate to this mode of talk. Thus while many communities have labels to apply to various linguistic practices at different levels which are evaluated as good or bad by the community – for example, 'grammatical', 'sloppy', 'drawl', 'h-dropping' – there seem to be very few or none which relate specifically to code-switching behaviour (although there are a few terms, such as 'Tex-Mex', which refer to mixed *varieties*). The few references to their own practices by members of code-switching communities which are contained in the literature are vague and general: for example, the now-famous quotation (complete with slip of the tongue) from a Spanish-English bilingual which gave Poplack's important 1981 article its title: 'Sometimes I start a sentence in Spanish y termino en Español' (Sometimes I start a sentence in Spanish and finish in Spanish). This lack of vocabulary acts as a further barrier to discussing code switching in any detail with linguistically naive members of the community.

The problem is compounded where the codes in contact themselves are not only similar but have diffuse norms, so that the boundary between them is not always clear either to the linguist or to community members. In the case of the Norwegian dialects studied by Blom and Gumperz (1972), a diglossic relationship existed between the two varieties. Thus although relatively few criteria may have held them separate in linguistic terms, for community members they were distinct, focused varieties with their own names and norms. This is not so obviously the case with Caribbean Creoles and English: though from the point of view of British English speakers Creole may be different from all British English varieties in salient ways, it is not clearly a separate language for members of the Creole-speaking community. Although British-born members of the community operate with the notion of two opposed varieties, 'Patois' and 'ordinary English' as we have seen, there is a lot of overlap. The question 'Were you speaking Patois or English just then?' will not necessarily make a lot of sense to a member of the London Caribbean community, any more than the questions 'Why did you say that in Patois?' or 'How would the effect of that be different if you said it in ordinary English?'.

A Conversation Analysis Approach to Code Switching

The difficulty of probing questions like those above with the help of community-member informants provides one incentive for using another approach: Conversation Analysis (CA), which has its roots in the tradition of sociology known as ethnomethodology. Ethnomethodology

> is an organizational study of a member's own knowledge of his ordinary affairs, of his own organized enterprises, where this knowledge is treated . . . as part of the same setting that it also makes orderable (Garfinkel 1974: 18)

For the conversation analyst's methodology (see e.g. Sacks et al. 1978; Heritage 1984; Levinson 1983), it is fundamental that the organisation of talk is structured rather than haphazard or accidental, and that no feature of talk can be dismissed a priori as irrelevant. Furthermore, participants in talk continually listen and respond to the talk of other participants, and in so doing, display their own analyses of what has gone before. It is these participant-analyses and only these which are accessible to the non-participant analyst. Hence,

> the methodology employed in CA requires evidence not only that some aspect of conversation *can* be viewed in the way suggested, but that it actually is so conceived by the participants producing it. That is, what conversation analysts are trying to model are the procedures and expectations actually employed by participants in producing and understanding conversation. (Levinson 1983: 318–19)

This means that for any claim by a researcher, a warrant must be produced by demonstrating a relevant response by the participants within the conversation itself. As Levinson (1983: 320–21) puts it,

> Conversation, as opposed to monologue, offers the analyst an invaluable analytical resource: as each turn is responded to by a second, we find displayed in that second an *analysis* of the first by its recipient. Such an analysis is thus provided by participants not only for each other but for analysts too.

The advantage of this approach is that the analyst's intuitive notions of 'what is going on' in the conversation do not occupy a central role, being replaced instead by an analysis of the talk in terms of other participants' reactions and responses. Such an approach is, of course, not exclusively suited for 'outsiders' analysing another community's talk: in fact, most studies of this kind have been by monolinguals studying conversations in their own or related dialects. There have been only a small number of studies which have applied these techniques to bilingual data, for example: Auer 1981, 1984a, 1984b; Auer and Di Luzio 1983a, 1983b; Tate 1984; Sebba and Wootton 1984; Milroy and Li Wei (forthcoming).

The type of analysis which this approach produces is necessarily somewhat different from that produced by other approaches. Many studies have aimed at typologies of code switching which classify switches according to their function in discourse. For example, Gumperz identifies the following functions (1982: 75–84): quotations (using a different code to mark a stretch of quoted speech), addressee specification (choosing a code to pick out one's intended addressee), interjections ('sentence fillers' offset from the the main content of the sentence by a code switch), reiteration (the message content is emphasised by repeating it in the other code), message qualification (the main content of the message is 'qualified' or adjusted by a clause in the other code), personalisation versus objectivisation. This last category Gumperz describes as

> somewhat more difficult to specify in purely descriptive terms. The code contrast here seems to relate to such things as the distinction between talk about action and talk as action, the degree of speaker involvement in, or distance from, a message, whether a statement reflects personal opinion or knowledge, whether it refers to specific instances or has the authority of a generally known fact. (Gumperz 1982: 80)

The difficulties inherent in a non-member of a speech community attributing motivations to community members' speech behaviour have already been mentioned. This is where the CA approach, requiring the analyst to display a 'warrant' for all claims in the form of participants' own responses, has an advantage. Although Gumperz bases his analyses on transcriptions of actual conversation, his examples consisting of 'illustrative brief exchanges, just long enough to provide a basis for context bound interpretation' (1982: 75) show only the stretches of speech containing the code-switched utterances themselves, and omit specifications of pauses, laughter, other parties' contributions which overlap with the current speakers' and other details which are considered potentially important by conversation analysts. (Thus Auer complains of Gumperz that 'sometimes he makes strong claims about the effect of a given type or instance of code switching on the subsequent development of the sequence, which are based on informants' reports, but fails to reproduce this subsequent passage' (Auer 1984b: 106, fn. 10).)

Gumperz approaches the pragmatics of code switching by looking at the *social* significance of each language or code, the *content* of the utterance and the *code* of that utterance. It is central to his thinking that for most communities, each code has its own symbolic value in terms of 'we' and 'they'. The 'we' code is generally that with the longer association with the community, the community's 'own' language, while the 'they' code is the community's 'new' language, a language of wider communication with the rest of the world. In code switching, the symbolic value of each language attaches to utterances in it, giving them their special meaning in context by contrast with an utterance with the similar content, but in the other code.

A conversation analytic approach to code switching, on the other hand,

> gives priority to dialogical meaning, that is, to meaning as a nego-tiated property of interaction. This is to say that linguistic (as well as social) activities become significant because they are given signi-ficance by all participants – not only the 'speaker'. Consequently, conversation analysis limits the external analyst's interpretational leeway because it relates his or her interpretations back to the members' mutual understanding of their utterances as manifest in their behaviour. 'Meanings' are neither equated with speakers' in-tentions, nor with recipients' interpretations; both are looked on as mental entities which are of little interest as long as they do not 'materialize' in interaction. (Auer 1984a: 6, footnote omitted)

Thus the 'meaning' of code switching, rather than arising out of community norms and being attributable by the analyst to in-dividual switches, is something actively constructed by partici-pants in the conversation, displayed by them through their responses, and available to the analyst through these displays only. The analysis 'provided by participants not only for each other but for analysts too' (in Levinson's words, quoted above) is thus the ultimate arbiter of the 'meaning' of code switching. As Auer puts it (1984a: 5), 'under close scrutiny, the details of the sequential embeddedness of language choice and language alter-nation permit us to formulate the coherent procedural model we are looking for'.

The attractions of the CA methodology in the study of code switching can be summarised as follows:

(1) The CA approach avoids premature theorising about what is or is not of interest to the analyst. A detailed transcription, making no *a priori* assumptions of what is relevant and what is not, is a prerequisite.
(2) The analyst must demonstrate a warrant for all claims, in the form of a sequential response within the talk itself.
(3) Hence the role of the analyst's own intuitions and external

'uncontrollable' factors is minimised; the analysis is based on what is *in* the talk and (in theory) nothing else.

A critique of CA

At this point it must be said that the CA methodology is not without its critics. In a detailed critique, Taylor and Cameron (1987: 117) point out that the CA approach makes

> the identification of conversational units dependent on the specification of the conversational rules to which speakers 'orient' in constructing sequences of such units. At its worst, this might sound like a circular method of analysis, setting up a prototypical chicken-and-egg dilemma.

However, they continue:

> But it may perhaps be better understood as an analytical consequence of the Garfinkelian theory that the fit between organization and phenomena, between rules and their applications, is not determined in advance, but rather is the result of an *ad hoc* and context-sensitive process, performed by speakers (by the use of shared 'methods'), in which the recognition of the social act and the construction of interpretation of sequences of such acts are two sides of the same creative (but nonetheless organized and accountable) process. (Taylor and Cameron 1987: 117)

Having countered their own criticism, however, they go on to argue (p.120) that CA's 'apparent analytical successes are dependent upon the analyst's stepping beyond the methodological limits allowed by the underlying ethnomethodological principles'. In their analyses of the understanding 'displays' of next turns, Cameron and Taylor argue, the conversation analysts fail to follow their own prescriptions, which require them to look to the participants' analysis displayed in the *next* turn. But this, Taylor and Cameron argue, 'rather than offering the analyst direct access to the participants' own publically displayed identification of units and rules, only postpones the task to a subsequent turn' (p. 121). Empirical evidence of the participants' interpretation of next turns is not available, and conversation analysts instead fall back on circular arguments, claiming that the conversation develops as it does by 'orientation' to the same organizational devices which have to be taken for granted in order to get this interpretation of the data (p. 120).

Taylor and Cameron's critique of CA methodology can be taken as a warning that purely ethnomethodological methods may not be enough to give a satisfying account of code switching. However, it can surely do no harm to apply these methods to code switching data, as long as the analyst is aware of the boundary between participants' *own* interpretations – as warranted by 'displays' within the talk – and the analysts' intuitive interpretations. This line is not always easy to draw. Nonetheless, I believe that the CA approach can get us further with the study of code switching than other approaches tried so far, and it is on that basis that I have chosen to use it in this book.

Code switching in practice

In what follows I shall give an account of selected aspects of the code switching behaviour of young British-born black people in London, based on conversational data collected mainly in family homes in the course of my research project (see Introduction). I do not believe that it is possible to produce a *predictive* model of code switching, in other words, to derive inductively a set of rules which would predict the actual code of any 'next utterance' in a conversation. What we can more profitably do is look at the way speakers *have* used code switches in the past, in an effort to understand their motivations.

Salient switches

Most conversational uses of Creole by British-born speakers are short, and embedded in longer stretches of British English. Extracts (1) and (2) below are examples.

Extract 1: Conversation B–1

> B   I wanna know say, this guy is an impen – independent guy
>   who can do fings on 'is own, I can't find
>   I can't find all that <u>shi%%eries in a day!</u>
> →   < "shitteries" = junk, nonsense>

Extract 2: Conversation D–3

1   V   oh it's a laugh is that one (0.8) watch * *
      <u>watch she a skyank!</u>
    < laughter (3.0)>
    V   did (did you leave) the radio on *? was the radio on?

These two extracts show some similarities. In each case, the
Creole comes at the end of the speaker's turn. In each case, it is
the Creole which is reacted to: in (1), by J, who responds 'you
can't', and in (2) by all the parties to the conversation, who laugh
for three seconds – rather a long laugh. The curious thing about
such stretches of Creole is that they are *never* treated as an invitation to continue the conversation in Creole, but rather as a
one-off comment. The next turn is always in British English,
possibly preceded by laughter. In some sense, then, the function
of the Creole seems to be to emphasise the content of that particular piece of talk, for it is that content which is reacted to by
other speakers. The Creole elicits a response to its content, but
does not elicit more Creole.

There are also clear differences between (1) and (2). Whereas
in (1) B's talk is received seriously – without laughter, in fact with
silence followed by supportive agreements – in (2), V's talk is met
with laughter and is clearly perceived as joking. Here we have at
least two different phenomena, which deserve separate study. Let
us take a closer look at each.

One-liners which get laughs

The frequency with which Creole utterances are met with
laughter in my conversational data is remarkable. This does not
mean, of course, that everything said in Creole is treated as a
joke. Rather, the use of Creole in a particular utterance *within a
particular type of sequence in conversation* may mark that utterance as requiring non-serious interpretation. We have already
seen two examples of this: the refusals from E–2 and Conversation J where a potentially face-threatening refusal was instead
treated as jocular and received with laughter.

Extract 3, from D–1, contains two 'jocular one-liners'.

Extract 3: Conversation D–1

C   no Laverne (0.1) Laverne you shouldn't take no more
        pictures like that of me

35 L   no, sorry right you didn't want me to take [tɛk] it over
        you right I just had to sneakup

V   You see (wha woman wear no)

< laughter (0.5)>

C   what was I ⌈ wearin'? that's Nicolette!

40 V   ⌊ * * * * * yeh look at her in her
        (sexy) jean guy (.) deadly!
        ʔeh heh

C   'n 'er trousers

45 L   hih that's me! (0.6) ⌈ <u>Valerie cut me off there <u>bwo::y</u>!</u>
C   ⌊ (must be the one in my bathroom)

V   no I never! It's just my wardrobe that's all

(1.0)

The three speakers are looking at photographs in an album. At
line 37 V interjects in Creole 'you see what the woman's wearing!' which is followed by laughter from the others. Following
the laughter C, who apparently cannot see the photograph, asks
'what was I wearing?': her London English response to the Creole
comment which elicited the laughter. L's utterance in line 45 begins with a comment on the photograph in London English
('that's me') but after a pause she switches to Creole to comment
on V's photography: 'Valerie cut me off there, boy!' which she
follows with a laugh. V's response is a denial – the expected response to an accusation – and is in London English: 'no I
never . . .'. The formula for both these jocular comments is
similar: in the midst of a conversation which has continued for at
least two turns in London English, a speaker introduces a turn
which ends in Creole (typically such turns are at most one sentence long, and wholly in Creole). This is followed by laughter.
The conversation then continues in LE. Examples similar to (3)
are to be found in many places in Conversation D: for example,
D–3, lines 1–3.

The effect of these personal remarks spoken in Creole is thus
rather like that of the 'jocular' refusals; potentially insulting on
the face of it, but in fact treated by all participants as not serious
and non-threatening.

Punch lines

Related to the 'joking' one-liners is a class of code switches called 'turn-final switches' by Sebba and Wootton (1984): less seriously we might call these 'punch lines'. In these the first part of a turn is in London English and the last part in Creole. The Creole part of the turn is treated by the speaker and other participants as being salient: it typically consists of a short stretch of Creole which brings the turn to a pointed conclusion, by summarising or reaffirming the speaker's main point. Although it is not accompanied by laughter either from the speaker or other participants, there is evidence that the other participants do treat the Creole material as the salient content of the turn by responding to that rather than some other part of it. This is the case in (1), where B's final sentence 'I can't find all that shitteries (= junk, stuff) in a day' is the portion of her turn responded to by her listeners, with a chorus of 'you can't' and 'sometimes it takes years'. This response of J's to the explicit time reference (to 'a day') embedded in the Creole part of B's turn is independent evidence of its salience for the other participants. The Creole portion is also somewhat louder and raised overall in pitch.

As in the case of the 'jocular comment', the speaker's switch to Creole does not provoke a Creole response. The conversation continues in London English as before and the Creole is treated as 'one off'.

In Extract 4, there is again a turn-final switch, but this time, the speaker builds up to it more clearly.

Extract 4: Conversation B–2

```
 1  B    'ang on a minute * I'll tell you now ⌈ * (anybody)
    ?                                        ⌊ it's wrong though
    B    goes to me, right, go outside for (me) freshair I don't
         wanna go outside for fresh air, right, me na go outside
 5       ⌈ for no fresh air
    J    ⌊ even if you do go out for fresh air it don't mean you're
         gonna have sex outside there
    L    hey it hot in 'ere you know Jane you wan' come outside ya
    J    * *
10       < all laugh>
```

According to Sebba and Wootton (1984: 7)

the turn-final Creole portion 'reinforces' something said immediately before in LE. The conversation is about how to respond to an invitation to 'step outside' at a party: the gist of B's turn is that if someone were to ask her to go outside for 'fresh air' at a party, she would not want to go outside for fresh air, and would not go. The way the turn is constructed is interesting. B begins by offering her view as something which should be of interest to the others: 'I'll tell you now': she had made several previous attempts to interrupt with 'let me tell you'. Next she places her story in the realm of the hypothetical: '(if) anybody goes to me . . .' The next part is a quotation of what the hypothetical invitation would sound like, and is characterised by a [Creole] pronunciation of the vowels in go and outside, though the phrase as a whole ('go outside for freshair') is not clearly marked as Creole.

Next B states, in London English, her attitude to all such propositions: 'I don't wanna go outside for fresh air, right' – and now switches to Creole to echo her own words, but more emphatically: not only would she not want to go, she *will not*: 'I'm not going outside (ever) for any fresh air'. The strengthened assertion ('won't' vs. 'wouldn't want to') and the build-up to a climax are already there in B's turn even without the code switch from London English to Creole: 'fresh air' is mentioned three times, each time with greater prominence than before, and the overall impression is of a crescendo which reaches its climax with the final *'fresh air'*. The Creole gives an added emphasis to the last part of the turn and marks its imminent end: this is shown by the reaction of the other speakers. J starts to speak in overlap with B as soon as B has spoken the main part of her Creole 'echo' sentence, *me na go outside* [line 4].

Example 5, from the same conversation, is rather similar in construction.

Extract 5: Conversation B-3

```
   T     * * * * * * 'is car, even if 'e's in 'is car, man
10→B     I wouldn't sleep in 'is car ⌈ me na sleep in 'is car for me have
   ?                                 ⌊ (see these people)
   B     me bed at home
   ?     ooh, ⌈ god
   T           ⌊ * there's a lo% of things might 'appen
   B     no, I don't business, no:!
```

Trevor, a male friend, is trying to persuade Brenda that if she let a man take her home they might sleep together. Brenda's initial response to Trevor's 'even if 'e's in is car, man' is the London English 'I wouldn't sleep in 'is car' (line 10): but she reaffirms this in Creole in the same turn (<u>me na sleep in 'is car</u>) and furthermore gives her reason: '<u>for me have me bed at home</u>'. Once again the progression is from 'wouldn't' in London English to 'am not' in Creole.

Mid-turn switches

There are other instances where the use of a stretch of Creole embedded in a basically London English turn serves to 'upgrade' the message content of the Creole stretch. One such example is (6), analysed at length by Sebba and Wootton (1984).

Extract 6: Conversation B–5

	B	then I just laughed (0.6) and then 'e – 'e just pulled me for a
15		dance – I didn't mind dancin' wiv 'im / 'cause <u>me know say,</u>
		<u>me no 'ave nothin' inna my mind</u> // but to dance, and then
		we star%ed to talk and all the rest of it /// and tha%'s it ////
		<u>full stop!</u>
	J	yeah
20	J	yeah
	J	yeah
	J	yeah
(2.0)		
	J	'e was a nice guy, but differently, right

Just before the start of this extract, Brenda has been talking with her friends about an incident at a party. Someone had mischievously told a boy that Brenda wanted him. Emboldened by this, he had gone straight up to her and said that he had heard she had called him and wanted him. Brenda tells her friends that she was shocked and responded by saying coldly 'did I really?' Her friends say she did the right thing. Brenda goes on to recount what happened after she rebuffed the boy in question. She agreed to dance with him because, she says, she knew she had nothing in mind but to dance (line 15–16): i.e. from her point of view it was all innocent and involved nothing more serious than dancing. The key statement of Brenda's turn is the one at line 15–16, which gives her explanation of why she agreed to dance with a man whose initial approach had shocked her and led her to respond coolly. Significantly, this statement of reasons is given in Creole. However, Brenda's turn is so constructed that it starts in London English with a statement about what happened, and switches to Creole at 'cause' (which could be London English or Creole) – precisely the point where she begins her explanation of why she acted in this way. Brenda continues in Creole until just before 'but to dance', then switches back to London English for the last part of her turn, where she continues with her narration of <u>actual</u> events: 'and then and then we star%ed to talk and all the rest of it and tha%'s it' – but switches to Creole for her final 'punchline': '<u>full stop</u>'.

Sebba and Wootton (1984: 6) write:

> The Creole stretch is distinguished from the rest of the turn structurally as well as in terms of its code. Brenda's turn is structured as a telling of a series of events which followed the initial exchange between her and the boy: '*then* I just laughed, and *then* 'e pulled me for a dance . . . and *then* we started to talk . . .' The longer stretch which contains the Creole part of the turn, beginning with 'I didn't mind' and ending 'but to dance' – disrupts this pattern and is thus set off from the rest of the turn. It strikes us as most interesting that this part of Brenda's turn begins and ends in London English, although the most essential part of it, the portion which describes Brenda's state of mind, is in Creole. It is as though Brenda 'works up to' the Creole portion and then 'comes down' to London English afterwards.

It is also interesting that three of the four responses from Jane which overlap with Brenda's talk in this turn exactly correspond to the points where she switches code. The same phenomenon can be seen in (5) where there is overlap beginning at the start of Brenda's Creole stretch in line 11. The fact that other parties respond at just these code switch points suggests that they represent the boundaries of salient categories within the talk – or putting it another way, that they represent the participants' perceptions of the relevant sections of talk which require or permit a response – even where these boundaries do not correspond with any syntactic boundary.

In Extract 7, from B–4, on the other hand, the overlapping

talk does not commence until after the first part of Brenda's Creole stretch.

Extract 7: Conversation B–4

```
 5   B   now 'e ad everyfing if you was to sit down an
             'ear that guy speak (.) ⌈ 'e (was going) to Jamaica
                                    ⌊ 'e was ni:ce (0.8) 'e was ni:ce
     B   'e was going to build 'is place (0.6)
         ⌈ 'im a build 'is business (1.0)
10   ?   ⌊ ye:h 'e was NI:CE man
     B   an' it's the type of guy like that (0.6) I ⌈ want
     ?                                             ⌊ yeah
    (0.6)
     B   ⌈ know what I mean? But there again, those things didn't even
15   ?   ⌊ * * * * * * * * * * * *
     B   ⌈ enter my mind turaatid!⌈
     ?   ⌊ * * * * * *
```

Brenda's turn beginning line 5 is constructed similarly to her turn in (6), with a Creole stretch in mid-turn. In one major respect it is different, though: her two pauses of 0.6 seconds (lines 11 and 13) are interpreted as signals that other speakers may now have the floor. Brenda is in competition with another speaker (most of whose words are inaudible) from then right up to the point where she winds up with her Creole 'punchline' *turaatid*, a mildish curse more or less equivalent to 'for god's sake'. The second part of the mid-turn switch itself also is overlapped by another speaker's 'ye:h 'e was NI:CE man'. So in spite of it being a mid-turn switch, in this case we seem to have a different type of switch from the one in (6), for the other parties to the conversation respond differently to it.

Insertions and interruptions: English within Creole turns

The switches we have looked at up to now have involved switches to Creole within a turn or sequence of turns in London English. Other types of switch involve a change of code from Creole to London English and back to Creole within a single turn. Such switches fall into two classes: 'speaker-initiated insertion sequences' and 'self-interruptions'.

Speaker-initiated Insertion sequences

Extract 8: Conversation C–2

```
       B   'ear 'im now no! he he
           (you) slap down
           'im say / 'pin' // (0.8) 'im slap down 'im say 'needle' ///
   5       'im slap down i what did you say again? (0.6) ///
           (0.8) what did you say?
       M   (pin)
       M   ha ha ha
       M   ha ha ha
  10   M   eh ha ha ha
       ?L  crablouse
```

We saw earlier that in the domino game, the preferred language was Creole by virtue of the presence of several Caribbean-
born and Creole-speaking players. Brenda used both Creole and
London English, code switching between the two. We also saw
that in C–1, Brenda commented on other players' actions in Creole (him tryina concentrate, etc.) while some of her questions addressed directly to the players were in London English, for
example: 'what does telephone mean, please?' In C–1, Brenda's
turns were constructed so as to be entirely in London English or
entirely in Creole.

In C–2, Brenda begins her turn in Creole with 'ear 'im now
no! ('Just listen to him!') followed by laughter. Now, consistent
with her previous practice of using Creole for comments in Creole on the other players, she begins to describe the players' code
words in turn – '(you) slap down, he says 'pin', he slaps down, he
says 'needle', he slaps down he –'.

All of this is in Creole, and is received with laughter by the
players. At this juncture Brenda appears to be unsure of the word
called by one of the players. This marks the point of her switch
to London English, which is not preceded by any pause or hesita-
tion marker: 'what did you say again . . . what did you say?'
She gets her reply from one of the players: 'crablouse' (said with
Creole pronunciation, but by a speaker who anyway has a Jamaican accent). Brenda now switches back to Creole by completing
her original sequence with the word she was missing, pronounced
as in Creole: crablouse.

The London English sequence here is clearly set off from the rest of Brenda's turn by its function, which is to elicit a 'lost' piece of information. Similar sequences, known as self-initiated insertion sequences, are common in the talk of monolinguals: 'self-initiated' because the current speaker starts them rather than being prompted by another, and 'insertion sequences' because they disrupt the 'normal' flow of the conversation. What is striking in this case is that the sequence is *also* clearly marked by a change of code from Creole to English.

Extract (9) is another example of this. In this case, Joan is merely checking with Carol about potentially shared information: whether Carol knows 'Johnny'. Again, this type of insertion sequence is common among monolinguals: here it is clearly offset by being in London English in the midst of a Creole turn.

Extract 9: Catford Girl's Possee

(See Chapter 2 for the full transcription.)

```
5  C   no, she invite (0.4) um (.) you know Johnny ?
   J   yeah
   C   him tell me (0.8) and my mum went to her house and she
       said (0.4)
       she's o- she just told 'er she's 'avin' a christenin' (0.2)
       me no know if me a go
```

What characterises these speaker-initiated insertion sequences, then, is that the London English part of the speaker's turn is a sequence embedded in the turn but not part of the mainstream; it does not necessarily start at a syntactic clause completion point (for example (8), where it begins after a subject pronoun) and its purpose is to elicit information, or check on information to make it possible for the speaker to complete the current turn (Sebba and Wootton 1984: 4).

(2) Self-interruptions

Another type of within-turn switch is similar to the last type except that the switch to London English and back occurs wholly within the turn of one speaker: they are thus 'self-interruptions' (Sebba and Wootton 1984: 4). These seem to have a 'psychological' motivation similar to that of the other type. An example is (10):

Extract 10: Catford Girl's Possee

(See Chapter 2 for the full transcription.)

```
      J    Leonie have party?!
15    C    man (1.0) Leonie have party (0.4) when? (1.2)
           don' remember when it was but she did tell all o' dem
           no fi- t say not'in' (0.6) cau' she no wan' too much
           Cyatford gyal de dere (1.0) an' Jackie 'ave one too
           (0.4) never say not'in'
```

Here, Carol is trying to recollect the date of the party she has just mentioned. Carol's turn at line 15 is punctuated by two pauses – a shorter one which marks the boundary of her Creole utterance, and a longer one after her question 'when?', which functions to show that she has 'lost' the date in her memory and needs time to think about it.

There is the possibility that at this point, Joan could interpret this as a genuine request for information addressed to her, and respond, for example, 'on Tuesday' or 'I don't know', creating an insertion sequence like that of (8) or (9). What actually happens is that Carol answers her own question – in London English, with 'don' remember when it was'. She then immediately switches back to Creole to 'link up' with the first part of her turn.

Again, self-interruptions of this type are common in monolingual speakers. They interrupt the speaker's 'flow' in exactly the same way. What is striking about these is that the code-switch points coincide exactly with the beginning and end of the insertion sequences, off-setting these clearly as London English in an otherwise Creole turn of the conversation.

Extract (11) is a very similar example, although less striking in that Brenda's turn begins in London English before switching to Creole and back to London English for the self-interruption:

Extract 11: Conversation G–2

```
1     B    Na:h (0.6) (up) (0.4) Tuesday 'e told
           whasisname (t) come – come phone me right (0.2) So me me –
→          (0.8) what 'appened u:m (0.2) yeah,
           so a phone Winston and tell Win- and tell Winston
5          (and) 'e goes to me 'e wants to go out (0.6)
```

Code Switching and narrative strategies

One function of code switching often mentioned in the literature is *quotation*. This *may* mean simply that a bilingual speaker will quote the actual words of another speaker in the original language. However, researchers now agree that the situation is more complex. Gumperz (1982: 82) points out, for example, that monolingual speakers are not always quoted in the language they normally use: he gives the example of a Slovenian bilingual quoting another Slovenian's talk in German. This point is further elaborated by Romaine (1989: 148–9), who writes: 'it is the switch itself which must be significant, rather than the accuracy of the representation of the reported speech with respect to its linguistic form'. Gumperz warns 'whatever patterning there is in this type of code switching cannot be explained by generalized rules relating conversational functions to instances of code use' (1982: 83).

'Quotation' thus seems to be a code-switching phenomenon which can work at several levels. On the one hand, we have examples of speakers self-quoting, where the act of quoting activates a switch back to the code of the original utterance.

Extract 12: Conversation A–1

```
      B    cause some of them you see, (.) outside the street, (.)
           right, ⎡ and you say 'da% is a halfcaste
     ?L           ⎣ an' you don' know you can't * *
  →   B    ⎡ an im stone black he he you know what I mean?
 15   F    ⎣ e:::: yeah yeah
  →   B    stone black
  . . .
  →   B    (well) I mean by stone black I mean their
 30        parents is
```

On another level, quotation may involve speakers straightforwardly reporting their own speech in the original code. This could be the case with Valerie's reported speech in D–2 and D–4:

Extract 13: Conversation D–2

```
 20   V    'how should I pose?' she's goin' to me
           I said 'pose anyhow'
      ?    eh he he
```

Extract 14: Conversation D–4

> V　I said to her (1.0) come and take a photograph
> 　　'Who me? you mad! Inna dis kinda state?'
> (0.8)　hhh < laughter (2.0)>
> V　I said to her 'pose anyhow' (1.5) 'She says 'is dis alright?'

The word 'pose' occurs frequently in Conversation D, often with its Creole pronunciation [pʊʒz]. A turn which contains the Creole pronunciation is often met with laughter, as in (13). In both (13) and (14) Valerie reports the exchanges as involving a change of codes between speakers: thus in (13) her cousin addresses her in London English but Valerie's response is in Creole. In (14) her mother uses Creole (and this is very clearly intended to be a direct quote, even a send-up, of her mother's refusal), while Valerie answers her in London English. If this *is* what actually happened, it falls in line with what we know about asymmetric use of Creole between parents and children in the community.

At yet another level, code switching in quotation is available as a narrative strategy, to off-set the quotation (direct or indirect) from the rest of the turn. In such cases the code used in the quotation need not be that used by the original speaker: its force derives from the fact that it is *different* from the code of the part of the turn in which it is embedded. Extract 15 illustrates this clearly.

Extract 15: 'Private lessons'

(Adele and Belinda. Recorded in a Catford school)

```
1  A   wha% was 'private lessons' like? (1.8)
   B   (nah) de boy experience ⎡ he::
   A                           ⎣    eheh: experience what?
5  B   * start now
   (4.0)

   A   I t'ink you did say you was going to see it dough
   (0.6)
   B   yeah, but we didn't catch out (2.8) you know 'cause I was
10      sick an' t'ing you know?
```

At line 7, Adele's indirect-speech report of what Belinda had said – 'you was goin' to see it' is in London English, while the surrounding talk of the turn is in Creole. The switch back to Creole for the single word 'though' is particularly striking. We can speculate that there is a psychological motive for this switch, with Adele using a change of code to indicate that she is only *reporting* these words and does not herself 'stand behind' them or vouch for their validity.

If this is right, then the last example invites comparison with an earlier one, Extract 6, where the speaker is again 'reporting' – only this time, her innermost thoughts, which she very much stands behind:

>   B   [then I just laughed (0.6) and then 'e – 'e just pulled me for
> 15   a dance – I didn't mind dancin' wiv 'im / 'cause <u>me know
>   say, me no 'ave nothin' inna my mind</u> // but to dance, and
>   then we star%ed to talk and all the rest of it /// and tha%'s
>   it //// <u>full stop</u>!
> (Extract 3: Conversation B–5)

Lastly, we find examples where code switching for 'quotation' combines with switching at other points in a narrative strategy. Extract 16 shows this:

Extract 16: The Difficult Customer

(Andrew aged fifteen, Barry aged sixteen. Andrew's parents are Jamaican (from St Andrews and Kingston) Barry's father is Barbadian and his mother is from the southern United States. Recording made in a school in South East London.)

> 1   A   yeah man, I was on the till on Saturday (1.2) and this this
>   black man <u>come</u> in (1.0) and (0.6) you know our shop, right,
>   (0.6) they u:m (0.2) give (.) refund on (0.3) Lucozade bottles
>   (0.4)
>   B   m:
> 5   A   a black man <u>come in an' 'im b(h)u::y</u> a bottle (.) of <u>Lucozade</u>
>   while 'e was in the shop ⌈ an'
>   B   ⌊ free p- e's e got free pee off is it?
>   A   yeah
>   B   small ones or big ones?

```
10  A    big ones and 'e drank the bottle in fron% of us an then
         ask(d) for the money back (see man) me want me money now
    B  ⌈ heheh
    A  ⌊ he goes (pnk) (I'm on) the till guy (.) hhh (I jus ) (0.6) I
         jus' look round at 'im (0.6) I said well you can't 'ave it (1.9)
15       I said I 'ave to open the till (w) wait till the next customer
         comes (1.0) 'now! open it now and give me the money' (1.0)
         I said I can't (0.8) the man just thump 'is fist down an' (screw
         up dis for me) (.) (s no man) the manager just comes (.)
         would you leave the shop
20       before I call the security: hh the man jus' take the bottle an'
         fling it at me an (I) jus' catch it at the (ground)
```

This is an example of how a speaker, by skilfully using code switches, can create or 'animate' a character within a narrative. The speaker is Andrew, a seventeen year-old boy of Jamaican parentage: the majority of the narrative is London English. The main character in the incident he relates is a black man. One might expect that the speech of both the narrator (who here has the role of shop assistant on till duty) and the obstreperous customer would both be reported in the same code: either London English or Creole, since both are young black Londoners. In fact, they are not. Andrew's own reported speech, like most of his narration, is in London English. The customer's is mostly in Creole, cf. lines 11 and 16, where the boundaries of the Creole stretches correspond with 'quotation marks'. However, there are other Creole stretches of talk in this narrative, especially lines 5, 17 and 20–21. (Note that *thump* [tɒmp] and *fling* are characteristically Creole words.) These Creole stretches are just those parts of the narrative where the customer himself and his actions are described: come in an' 'im b(h)u::y, just thump 'is fist down, jus' take the bottle an' fling it at me, all of which have 'the man' as subject.

Although the correspondence between the use of Creole and the description of the customer's actions is not perfect, what the narrator seems to be doing is creating a persona for his character 'the difficult customer' by linking him to Creole. The impersonation of the shop manager at lines 19–20, done in a near-RP 'posh' voice, is an even clearer evocation of a persona, but this time using a maximally Standard style.

Another example of this is an extract already discussed above in the section on 'mid-turn switches'.

```
     B    'e was going to build 'is place (0.6)
        ┌ 'im a build 'is business (1.0)
10   ?  └ ye:h 'e was NI:CE man
     B    an' it's the type of guy like that (0.6) I want
```
(*Extract 7: Conversation B-4*)

Brenda is describing a certain man who is the type that she would like to marry. She begins her descripton of his plans in London English: '('e was going) to Jamaica, 'e was going to –'. At this point she switches to Creole: *'build 'is place, 'im a build 'is business*, and then returns to London English to describe her own attitude: 'an' it's the type of guy like that . . . I want'.

Commenting on this, Sebba and Wootton (1984: 8) write:

> The switch to Creole occurs before the first instance of 'build 'is' and this could be taken as a direct quotation of the man's words, rendered in Creole because he is apparently a Jamaican: cf. Brenda's 'if you was to sit down an' 'ear that guy speak'. More interestingly, however, this switch somehow indexes a culture for which this goal stands as an ideal: building your own place is a plausible goal in the Jamaican culture but very unusual in Britain, especially for a black person.

Again in this we have a speaker creating a 'persona' by the use of code switching. In both the instances we have looked at, the speaker uses the change of code to animate a persona which is not his/her own, but that of a character in a narrative. If this is possible, then it should also be possible for speakers to use code switching as a means to change their *own* personas in the course of conversation.

A possible example of this is in Extract 17.

Extract 17: Conversation F-1

```
1    L    where's my mini?
       (0.4)
     V    wha% mini? (2.2)
     L    see you (say you) don't know no mini the ** mini that I wore
5         there (* * drink * *)
       (8.0)
```

```
        L    (get murder) guy!
  →     V    I do:nt knoh where it is! (1.4) see it there?
        L    caught you (frown) didn't I?
  10    V    ha ha ha ha ha hi hi hi ha::: < laughter (4.6)>
       (3.4)
        V    ah?
        L    (shi:t) Valerie!
  15→   V    What? Whe you a call me name for?
       (0.4)
        L    Look in the wardrobe to see whether you see it
        V    see wha:%
       (0.4)
  20    L    ME MINI:!  ⌈ please
        V            ⌊ yer mini yer mini (0.2) twix' yer legs
        L    yeah * *
```

The interaction between Valerie and Laverne is in London English until the point where Valerie responds in vexation, 'I do:nt knoh where it is' with an open back rounded vowel in both 'do:nt' and 'knoh' – pronunciations more characteristic of Creole than London English. The irritation is evident not only from Valerie's switch to a more Creole-like phonology but also from the intonation and amplitude of her response. The same is true of her Creole response (line 15) to Laverne's calling her name, to which Laverne responds, deferentially, by using London English. Valerie's irritation, whether actual or feigned, is linked to expression in Creole. What seems to be happening is that Valerie is adopting a 'Jamaican' persona in which irritation may be shown more freely (but also, perhaps, less threateningly) to a person's face. This could also be the motive behind the Creole refusals of requests which were discussed earlier.

'We' and 'They' Code Revisited

The Conversation Analytic approach to code switching taken here relies on the responses of the participants in a conversation to warrant claims about the work which a particular code switch is doing. Other approaches, such as that of Gumperz (e.g. 1982), tend to use intuitive categories as a basis for a description of code switching, relying on notions of psychological motivation to account for particular switches. This is *prima facie* convincing in the case of some communities, where a rigid diglossia obtains. For Gumperz is able to draw a distinction between a 'we' code, used in the family, the village, or among peers, and a 'they' code, which is used to talk to outsiders, on official business, in encounters outside the community, etc.

Among the Caribbean community in London the situation is ceratinly not so simple. Both London English and Creole are 'we' codes; both are used in the home and among peers and for discussing the most intimate subjects. Code switching in this community therefore does not immediately lend itself to an account based on a notion of 'we' and 'they': the 'we' and 'they' psychology must first be shown to exist.

An alternative approach, the one adopted here, is to examine in close detail the types of interaction which involve code switching, and to try to establish a taxonomy on the basis of these.

It is interesting and perhaps methodologically important that the Conversation Analytic approach tentatively provides support for the 'we code'/'they code' distinction, independently of 'given' notions of 'we' and 'they'. Sebba and Wootton (1984: 8–9) concluded on the basis of London English/Creole switching data which they studied, that there was a tendency for speakers to use a switch from Creole to London English within a turn 'to change from the main theme of the conversation to some kind of subroutine or secondary material: a check on shared information, a search for a missing name or date, a comment indicating how the acjacent material should be interpreted.' The London English code seems to be favoured for asides and insertions. On the other hand, stretches of Creole embedded in a London English turn often correspond to the most salient parts of the utterance, those which the other parties to the conversation respond to. If the 'we' code is taken to be the one which is closer to the 'heart and mind' of the speaker, and hence the one which imparts greatest salience to a given message, then Creole, even though used sparingly, does indeed seem to fulfil the 'we code' function for speakers in this community.

8 The Many-Personed Speaker

Young black Londoners are linguistically versatile. To start with, they usually have a command of at least two language varieties, Creole and British English. Within each of these varieties, there is a range of styles which the speaker can draw on in conversation or for other types of talk. In addition, there is dynamic interaction between the two varieties, mainly through code switching. Within individual conversations, speakers may 'negotiate' a level of Creole and British English usage with which they are comfortable.

Put this way, it makes the adolescent speakers described sound like adept linguists, at least with respect to a monolingual norm. Who, apart from speakers born into a bilingual community of this particular sort, would have, or be able to have, such a linguistic range and to perform so many delicate acts of linguistic negotiation in day-to-day interaction? But to take this line is to attribute to bilinguals special linguistic powers not shared by monolinguals. While I do not want to detract from the bilinguals' versatility or the value of their multicultural experience, I will argue in this chapter that in fact monolinguals have broadly the same range of linguistic 'powers' as bilinguals have, though sometimes these are manifested in other ways. In denying that bilinguals are special in this respect, I am arguing for an approach to the study of linguistic interactions which bridges the old barrier between 'variationist' studies, which deal with social and stylistic variation in 'monolingual', socially stratified speech communities, and 'ethnographic' studies of code switching and related phenomena which are normally confined to bilingual or diglossic bidialectal communities.

Variation and Identity

One of the chief foci of sociolinguistic interest in *monolingual* speakers is variation. Variation seems to affect all languages and to be present at all levels, although some language types, such as Creoles with post-Creole continua, seem to display more variation than others.

'Variationist' linguistics comes in several variants itself. The studies of Labov, Trudgill and Milroy use statistical measurements of phonological variables (typically, vowels and/or consonants) and establish correlations between these and external factors such as social class (e.g. Labov 1966, Trudgill 1974), social network (e.g. Milroy 1980), age and/or gender. Within this 'quantitative paradigm' (see Romaine 1982), it is assumed that variability is inherent in language and 'variable rules' give the best account of the frequency with which one or other variant is used within a particular group. In Labov's view, for example, 'the locus of language is in the community or group, and . . . the speech of any social group will be less variable than the speech of any individual.' (Romaine 1982: 244). Other researchers like Bickerton and Bailey work within a 'dynamic paradigm' where it is assumed that 'the individual is homogeneous and that variability results from the aggregation of internally consistent lects which are different from each other with respect to one or more linguistic features' (Romaine 1982: 11).

In both the quantitative and dynamic paradigms, measurements of grammatical and phonological variants are made across relatively large samples of speech (or occasionally, written text – e.g. Romaine 1982) without attention to the interactional context of individual occurrences of each variable. Within the quantitative framework, the instances of each variant are usually simply added up to produce a gross sum. This provides a measure of each speaker's variability with respect to the particular variants under consideration, but provides no clue as to why the speaker might have used the variant that he/she did in any particular case.

Work by social psychologists like Giles and his associates on the other hand, has focused on variation in individuals across different encounters. 'Accommodation theory' demonstrates that speakers adjust their speech in various ways to make it more similar or dissimilar to that of their interlocutors (see Giles and

Smith 1979 for a review.) Whether 'convergence' or 'divergence' takes place is dependent mainly on the relationship between the participants in the encounter, including factors such as the setting (institutional or informal), relative status, prior acquaintance, etc. Accommodation theory takes a range of variation as a given part of each speaker's competence; it seeks to relate some or all of this variation to the relationship between particular interlocutors.

A third approach, that of Le Page and Tabouret-Keller, also treats the individual speaker as the focus of interest, but regards the relationship between the individual and his/her (perceived) community or communities as the key factor influencing linguistic behaviour. In their terms, each linguistic act is an 'act of identity' by which the speaker demonstrates his/her group allegiances. Thus, 'the individual creates for himself the patterns of his linguistic behaviour so as to resemble those of the group or groups with which from time to time he wishes to be identified, or so as to be unlike those from whom he wishes to be distinguished' (Le Page and Tabouret-Keller 1985: 181)

On the face of it, this is similar to accommodation theory: speakers approximate their interlocutors' linguistic behaviour, or distance themselves from it, depending on whether or not they wish to identify themselves with that individual. But Le Page and Tabouret-Keller's hypothesis is not primarily concerned with interaction between an individual speaker and an interlocutor, although this might follow from it as a special case. Rather, speakers are seen as modifying their behaviour to accommodate to group norms, where *both the group and the norms themselves are as perceived by the speaker*. 'Groups', then, are creations of the speaker and may or may not correspond to 'groups' which would be identified by sociologists or anthropologists: in the words of Benedict Anderson (1983) in a related context, they are 'imagined communities'.

Furthermore, the individual speaker's ability to carry out successful linguistic 'acts of identity' is subject to a number of limitations:

> We can only behave according to the behavioural patterns of groups we find it desirable to identify with to the extent that:
> (i) we can identify the groups
> (ii) we have both adequate access to the groups and ability to analyse their behavioural patterns

(iii) the motivation to join the groups is sufficiently powerful, and
       is either reinforced or reversed by feedback from the groups
(iv)   we have the ability to modify our behaviour

(Le Page and Tabouret-Keller 1985: 182)

In contrast with Accommodation Theory this approach tries to relate the linguistic behaviour not just of two interacting individuals relative to each other, but of individuals with respect to the communities in which they find themselves. What is more, it is the individual speakers themselves who 'identify the groups' on which they model their behaviour: the groups are thus the speakers' own creations, not the creations of analysts. In this, the Le Pagean approach is compatible with the tenets of ethnomethodology (see Chapter 7).

Each of the three approaches discussed so far is an attempt to explain the similarities and differences between individuals' speech behaviour, even within what may be broadly construed as the same 'speech community'. However, each approach has its problems and limitations. The accommodation model deals with the adjustments which speakers make with respect to each other in a particular encounter, but it cannot explain the 'base line' of behaviour which each individual brings to that encounter, i.e. the speaker's own norm, which is itself somehow related to the community's norm. Quantitative variationist sociolinguistics is concerned with explaining community norms, but because of the statistical nature of its approach variants are 'counted in' without reference to their non-linguistic context. Generally, there is no analysis of the local conditions which produce this variation within an individual speaker's conversation.

Comparing the approaches of accommodation theory and variationism, we find that the first is concerned with the pattern of speakers' behaviour in particular encounters, the second with the overall trends of variability and changing norms within a community. The Le Pagean 'acts of identity' approach meanwhile insists on the importance of the individual as the locus of linguistic variation, and seeks through identifying the individual's group allegiances to relate individual variation to community norms. In practice though, research within this framework has concerned itself with 'patterns of linguistic behaviour' as made manifest, for example, through narrative or in interviews, rather than looking in detail at conversational encounters. The 'act of identity' is thus construed *broadly* as a pattern of behaviour over a largish domain, rather than, say, as an instant in the production of talk, where a choice between two phonetic realisations of the same phoneme is required.

Ideally, an approach is required which will narrow the focus of the 'act of identity' in such a way that individual choices like the one just mentioned can be seen as part of systematic behaviour patterns which are simultaneously typical of speakers' own fictive speech communities and conditioned by the immediate context of the interaction in which they occur. Such an approach would be able to take both style shifting and code switching into account, whether in monolinguals or bilinguals; and could relate both of these, as well as other discourse related phenomena, to wider 'patterns of linguistic behaviour' in the community. While such an approach should be equally applicable to the monolingual and bilingual situations, a code switching community would be a convenient place for testing hypotheses, since it would provide examples of different but potentially related dimensions of variation: stylistic, within each language, and code switching, between languages.

Variation and style

Bell (1984) points to two categories of extralinguistic factors which variationist sociolinguists have identified as correlating with linguistic variation. The first of these, the social dimension, 'denotes differences between the speech of different speakers', while the stylistic dimension 'denotes differences within the speech of a single speaker' (Bell 1984: 145). Bell draws attention to a difference of focus between variationists, who have dealt in 'narrow categories' or 'small-scale linguistic variables', and 'ethnographers, discourse analysts and so forth' who have dealt in broad categories, for example qualitative phenomena such as turn-taking, politeness strategies and address systems. (Bell 1984: 146–7). This concentration on broad or narrow, 'micro' or 'macro', Bell says, is true for both the social and stylistic axes of variation.

Herein lies a paradox: for in examining 'micro' variables (for example, two variant pronunciations of the vowel sound of *house*), variationists draw conclusions about the social stratification of a whole speech community; whereas by focusing on the 'macro' parameters of language choice and sequentiality in turn-taking, researchers like Auer draw conclusions about the motivation for an individual linguistic event – a particular code switch in a particular conversation.

The study of variation within a bilingual community introduces complexities which may not be apparent in what is construed to be a single monolingual 'speech community' like Labov's New York City. Indeed, such communities may not be typical of communities as a whole: Romaine (1982) regards it as certain that linguistic and social factors do not often interact straightforwardly in the way Labov suggests. The same can then be said of social and stylistic factors. Bell expresses the connection between these as 'an axiom of sociolinguistic structure', which he calls the Style Axiom:

> Variation on the style dimension within the speech of a single speaker derives from and echoes the variation which exists between speakers on the 'social' dimension. (Bell 1984: 151)

Bell goes on to make explicit a relationship between monolingual stylistic variation and bilingual behaviour:

> having two discrete languages available rather than a continuum of styles simply throws into sharper focus the factors which operate on monolingual style shift. The social processes are continuous across all kinds of language situations. What we may loosely term the formal/informal continuum is simply expressed in different code sets in different societies: by language choice in bilingual societies, by dialect switching in diglossic situations, and by style shift in monolingual societies. (Bell 1984: 176)

This is simply not adequate as an account of code switching behaviour of the sort described in this book. Even assuming that 'language choice' somehow subsumes code switching in non-diglossic situations, there seems to be no way of relating code switching behaviour directly to the 'social' dimension. While it may be true that the highest socioeconomic group uses nothing but Standard English, it is certainly not true that the lowest group uses only Creole, and that the middle classes are those who tend to switch between the two. This type of situation may exist in other cases of language interaction, but it is not universal: in any event, the model seems 'leaky' and has yet to be demonstrated to be valid in any bilingual community where code switching occurs.

Nevertheless, Bell is right in pointing out that style shift and code switching are closely related. Both involve a projection of the self *vis-à-vis* an interlocutor (or audience), as Bell demonstrates. And both may be the result of a change of *footing*, to which we now turn.

Footing

Within a single interaction – say, a conversation – participants need not maintain an unvarying relationship among each other, the linguistic event, and the context (both wide and narrow) in which it takes place. Indeed, if we take that conversation, as it unfolds, as constantly changing and renewing its own context, then the relationship just described *must* be constantly changing as well.

Much, perhaps most, of an individual's variation *within* a particular linguistic interaction may be associated with this changing relationship.

Goffman's notion of *footing* seems to come closest to encapsulating the complex of participant-oriented factors which are involved. As Goffman puts it (1981: 128), 'A change in footing implies a change in the alignment we take up to ourselves and the others present as expressed in the way we manage the production or reception of an utterance. A change in our footing is another way of talking about a change in our frame for events.'

Summarising 'roughly' the content of this notion, Goffman writes:

(1) Participant's alignment, or set, or stance, or posture, or projected self is somehow at issue.
(2) The projection can be held across a strip of behavior that is less long than a grammatical sentence . . . Prosodic, not syntactic, segments are implied.
(3) A continuum must be considered, from gross changes in stance to the most subtle shifts in tone that can be perceived.
(4) For speakers, code switching is usually involved, and if not

this then at least the sound markers that linguists study: pitch, volume, rhythm, stress, tonal quality.

(5) The bracketing of a 'higher level' phrase or episode of interaction is commonly involved, the new footing having a liminal role, serving as a buffer between two more substantially sustained episodes. (Goffman 1981: 128)

Each change of footing, then, can provide the occasion for a small 'act of identity' whose linguistic consequences, if any, become part of the new context in which the interaction is taking place. Goffman's notion of 'footing' thus mediates between changes of 'projected self' and its linguistic correlates, code switching and other 'sound markers that linguists study' – for example, perhaps, those that characterise style shift.

Persona

One among several identifiable functions of code switching in the British Caribbean community is *personation* – creating or evoking a character by the use of a particular speech style embedded in talk in another style. For example, the 'difficult customer' in Chapter 7, whose *actions* were presented in Creole by the narrator:

2	this this black man <u>come</u> in (1.0)
5	a black man <u>come in an'</u> 'im b(h)u::y a bottle (.) of <u>Lucozade</u>
10	and 'e drank the bottle in fron% of us an then ask(d)
17	I can't (0.8) the man <u>just thump 'is fist down</u>
20	the man <u>jus' take the bottle an' fling it at me</u> an (I) jus' catch it at the (ground)

Meanwhile, in the same narrative, the 'Creole' voice is also used to represent the 'difficult customer's' *own* words:

| 15 | for the money back (see man) <u>me want me money now</u> comes (1.0) <u>'now! open it now and give me the money'</u> (1.0) |

while a 'respectable' near-RP voice is given to the manager:

| 18 | the manager just comes (.) 'would you leave the shop before I call the security' hh |

For this kind of complex evocation to be effective in multi-party talk (such as conversation), the participants must share at least some of the speaker's perceptions about the speech styles in question: in other words, the evocation of a persona is dependent to some extent on the existence of shared stereotypes among the parties to the talk. As a speaker switches from animating one persona to animate another, the effect at the linguistic level may, for a bilingual speaker, be a code switch. For a monolingual speaker, it may mean a shift of style within what is perceived to be the same language.

In cases like the 'difficult customer', where the persona created is clearly not that of the narrator, it is easy to see how the change of code is part of the construction of a 'character' separate from the speaker. In other cases, however, the 'character' so constructed may be simply 'another self'. This could be the case, for example, in Conversation F-1 where Valerie assumes a Creole-speaking persona when she expresses irritation.

```
1    L   where's my mini?
     (0.4)
2    V   wha% mini? (2.2)
......
14   L   (shi:t) Valerie!
15→ V   What? Whe you a call me name for?
```

This suggests that speakers do more than simply animate a *persona* now and again for narrative purposes: they actually switch 'selves' from time to time, depending on 'who' they want to be at a particular moment, relative to their interlocutor.

This brings us back to Le Page's hypothesis: 'the individual creates for himself the patterns of his linguistic behaviour so as to resemble those of the group or groups with which from time to time he wishes to be identified'; only now we can treat 'linguistic behaviour' at a micro level, interpreting 'from time to time' to mean even at different stages within the same conversation – perhaps even the same utterance.

This ties in well with Goffman's ideas about changes of footing within talk. 'When we shift from saying something to reporting what someone else said, we are changing our footing. And so, too, when we shift from reporting our current feelings, the feelings of the "addressing self", to the feelings we no longer espouse. (Indeed, a code switch sometimes functions as a mark of this shift)' (1981: 151).

We can now see persona as a socially negotiated, linguistically realised manifestation of 'footing', animated by the speaker and mediated by the speaker's existing stereotypes (at least partially shared by other participants in the interaction.) Code switches or style shifts often (though not always) mark changes of persona and hence changes of footing within the conversation. In accordance with the principles of conversation analysis, the analyst should be able to demonstrate this in each case, by showing a response on the part of an interlocutor.

On this view, now, conversation consists of a series of sequential 'personations' by a speaker. Each time s/he utters a sound, s/he has a choice of which 'identity' to assume, which persona to animate, which 'character' to be. Where bilingual code switching is concerned, this is at its most obvious to the analyst. However, even in monolinguals, dramatic changes of persona are quite possible. Goffman (1981: 150) cites one type of example:

> if someone repeatedly tells us to shut the window, we can finally respond by repeating his words in a strident pitch, enacting a satirical version of his utterance ('say-foring'). In a similar way we can mock an accent or dialect, projecting a stereotyped figure more in the manner that stage actors do than in the manner that mere quotation provides . . . Interestingly it seems very much the case that in socializing infants linguistically, in introducing them to words and utterances, we from the very beginning teach them to use talk in this self-dissociated, fanciful way.[1]

At this point we may ask how it is that speakers go about creating *linguistically* the persona which they animate at any one particular time.

Putting this another way, what is the mechanism whereby we 'create . . . the patterns of . . . linguistic behaviour so as to resemble those of the group or groups with which from time to time [we wish] to be identified'? We are forced to assume (and this is the second of Le Page's riders to his hypothesis) that individual speakers perform an analysis of some sort on the linguistic behaviour of the 'group' they wish to identify with. Researchers within the tradition of accommodation theory have been most active in looking at the detail of 'monolingual' interactions in an attempt to see exactly what it is that speakers are doing.

Coupland (1984) studied the linguistic behaviour of a travel agency worker, 'Sue'. The percentages of certain socially significant variables in Sue's speech were compared with the percentages in the speech of her customers, who came from a wide social spectrum. Coupland reports (1984: 60):

> As percentages of the less-standard variants of each variable rise in the client's speech (as we move from occupation class I to V), so the percentages of these variants in Sue's speech in conversation with these groups generally rise. Indeed, a very similar pattern of covariation emerges with educational background as the criterion for establishing client subgroups. The percentages of variants in Sue's speech provide a reasonably reliable index of the socioeconomic status and educational background of her interlocutors, just as the percentages of those forms in the clients' own speech are able to do.

Making the reasonable assumption that Sue wanted, for professional reasons, to be 'identified with' her clients, we have here evidence that she *did* adjust her linguistic behaviour in such a way as to bring it closer to that of a group with which, at the time in question, she wished to be identified. (In fact, although Sue's speech covaried with that of her clients, she varied over a narrower range. This could be taken as showing limitations on her ability to converge completely – cf. Le Page's fourth rider.) Looking at this another way, we could say that Sue, in the course of her working day, altered her linguistic persona on many occasions in order to present the persona most appropriate to her dealings with her current interlocutor. The gross statistics of variation do not, of course, tell us exactly when (or why) these changes of footing happened, but they do provide evidence that they took place.

We can now turn to another question: how is it that Sue was able to covary so accurately with the speech of her interlocutor? Unfortunately we do not have a detailed, turn-by-turn transcription of her interactions, but it is reasonable to assume that her linguistic accommodation was preceded by an assessment of how her interlocutor might be *expected* to talk; in other words, that Sue's assumption of a persona would be mediated through a stereotype of the linguistic behaviour of the group to which she felt her customer belonged. This stereotype need not be wholly linguistic, indeed, according to Bell (1984: 168) 'Speakers are in fact able to respond to personal characteristics alone, when speech differs from a speaker's expectations of a given addressee.'

Bell cites experimental evidence reported by Beebe (1981) where Thai/Chinese bilinguals shifted consistently in the direction of Chinese-influenced vowel variants when interviewed by an ethnic Chinese, even though 'this represented divergence from the addressee's own speech. Such accommodation responds to what the speaker mistakenly assumes will be the addressee's speech on the basis of the addressee's non-speech attributes.'(Bell 1984: 168) In the case of Sue the travel agent, her convergence was 'successful' (Thakerar et al. 1982) in that she correctly assessed her interlocutors' speech behaviour and was able to converge towards it. Beebe's experiment suggests, however, that 'convergence' may involve a kind of personation – adopting what the speaker believes to be the speech characteristics of the interlocutor, rather than 'mirroring' speech forms already used by the interlocutor.

If the latter were the case, we would expect no accommodation to take place for a specific variable until that variable had already been used by the interlocutor. In other words, only when speaker 1 had heard speaker 2 pronounce a variable using a particular variant, would speaker 1 know that speaker 2 favoured that particular variant. Speaker 1 could then accommodate by using that variant back to speaker 2: though this would only appear as convergence where speaker 1 would 'normally' use that variant less than speaker 2. It is an empirical matter to determine whether or not this happens in practice. Even if it does happen, it does not force the conclusion that speaker 1 has monitored speaker 2's speech and made an assessment of how often speaker 2 uses that variant. Some or all of the 'convergence' could still be accounted for in terms of speaker 1's stereotype of how speaker 2 'should' sound.

Towards a 'micro' ethnographic sociolinguistics

Taking stock of some of the ideas discussed above, we can speculate that individuals, when they speak, adopt a particular posture or footing in relation to their interlocutor or audience; and that each *footing* in turn is associated with a persona, a 'someone' who that speaker is 'being' at that particular moment. This is especially clear in the case of bilinguals who code switch, whose personas may be indexed – though only in a gross way – by language. The persona, in turn, may represent a fictive group who the speaker 'wants to be like' at that particular moment; or rather, who the speaker wants to *appear* to be like; in terms of speech, wants to *sound* like. To animate a particular persona linguistically, a speaker must be able to access a stereotype of the persona's group; and in doing this, the speaker acts within certain constraints: Le Page's 'four riders', which limit the speaker's effectiveness in evoking the desired persona at any one moment. Our personas will be more or less realistic depending on how well we can identify their prototypes, and how linguistically adept we are at mimicking them.

If what has been hypothesised so far is true, much of the variation in linguistic interactions which is not explicable in terms of grammatical or phonological conditioning can be accounted for by changes of footing, involving a switch from one (linguistic) persona to another; some can be accounted for by the speaker's failure to identify perfectly the speech patterns of the prototypes of the personas which s/he seeks to animate at a particular time; and some can be accounted for by the speaker's imperfect ability to reproduce those speech patterns which s/he has identified. These last two factors introduce an element of randomness which means that a predictive theory would probably be impossible to construct, assuming that was what one wanted to do.

In the case of the London Caribbeans, we can say that their repertoire of personas includes some which are unambiguously London and some which are unambiguously Caribbean, as well as some which are not clearly one or the other. Elsewhere in this book I have identified a range of features – phonological, lexical and grammatical – which are characteristic of 'London English' or of 'Creole'. Much of the language behaviour of the speakers described in this book can be characterised as code switching between those two systems, but it is also clear that 'English' and 'Creole' interact at many other levels, both for these speakers and for the community as a whole.

At the phonological level, for example, we find Creole words like *picky-picky*, 'frizzy', are used within London English, their pronunciation 'nativised', while elsewhere we find the London pronunciations <u>breaf</u> and <u>frough</u> (/bref/ and /fru:/ for /breθ/ and /θru:/) within stretches of speech in other ways clearly marked as Creole. At the level of grammar we found that the Creole <u>say</u> can replace *that* within what is otherwise 'ordinary' British English, yet at the same time British English past tense markers may appear on 'Creole' verbs. This suggests that a fusion of languages is taking place which cannot be explained simply by an appeal to the notion that speakers from time to time animate different personas, some 'British' and some 'Caribbean'. But this is exactly what we might have expected: with the emergence of the black British identity has come a matching linguistic persona, neither London nor Jamaican, but 'London Jamaican'.

To conclude: I have suggested that conversational interactions, not just for speakers who obviously 'straddle two cultures' but even for those who have traditionally been called 'monolingual' and 'monocultural', involve the speaker in animating a series of personas which are realised linguistically and derive their symbolic value from their association with stereotypes which have reality and symbolic value for the interactants. Such personations may operate at several levels, so that the speaker may create a persona for another individual who is talked about, while at the same time animating several personas which represent him or her self. Linguistic representations of different 'selves' and 'others' are thus woven by a speaker into a complex skein of conversation (or narrative), with feedback from other interactants at all times potentially affecting the blend.

Linguistically, one outcome of all this is variation, at both a micro- and a macro-level. The characterisation of black London speakers as users of just two or three 'codes' is therefore too crude, although it is a useful model. Speakers have a wide range of variables at their disposal, and a wide range of personas to 'be' linguistically at any one time. In this respect, black Londoners, though interesting, are not unique.

Note

1. Variation in the speech of quite young children is well documented, cf. Romaine (1984: 100): 'If we take the term monostylistic to mean that there is little or no variation we would certainly not be justified in applying it to the speech of these children [= Edinburgh primary school children].'

9 EPILOGUE: Creole and the future – a language of education?

More than a decade after the first reports of 'London Jamaican' from Rosen and Burgess and D'Costa, we may look back at the questions which could not be answered at that time, and see what progress has been made. Research already described in this book, taken together with the work of others like Sutcliffe, Edwards, Hewitt and Tate, enables us to say at least the following:

(1) D'Costa's assertion that JC is 'an identifying group dialect common to all West Indians' is correct – provided we limit it to those born in Britain, i.e. nearly all adolescents and young adults. It is also necessary to use the term 'JC' cautiously. Though black adolescents are modelling their 'black talk' on JC rather than some other Caribbean variety, the norms for indigenous British Creole are different from those of Jamaica.

(2) The JC spoken by young blacks in Britain does appear to vary geographically, due at least to some extent to influence from the local variety of British English. The Bradford Rastafarians studied by Tate (1984) seem to be unique among the groups studied, inasmuch as their JC seems to carry no hint of Bradford English syntax or pronunciation. Other speakers may have readily identifiable local features but the differences are not ever likely to be great enough to make the varieties mutually unintelligible.

(3) The pull of JC for British-born black youth seems to outweigh the attraction of any of the other Caribbean Creole varieties spoken by the first generation. While fluency in this Creole may correlate somewhat with coming from a Jamai-

can background, Jamaican descent is clearly not a necessary condition for acquiring a command of JC, as shown by Tate's Dominicans. Some white Creole speakers in London seem to have competence in Creole on a par with black speakers who have average fluency in Creole: this is borne out by Hewitt's research (1982, 1986).

(4) With the possible exception of certain groups where Creole is in constant use in the home, e.g. among Rastafarians, all British born Caribbeans now have a variety of British English as their first language. The degree of competence which individuals reach in Creole depends very largely on their patterns of socialisation in childhood and adolescence. This may be related to the number of black children of the same age group in the individual's neighbourhood or class at school, and more generally, to the density of Caribbean settlement in the area. Edwards (1986) showed that in the West Midlands competence in Creole, and patterns of language use for Caribbean speakers, are strongly related to social network in this way. Hewitt makes a similar observation regarding London:

it appears that demographic factors are influential. In the areas of densest black settlement the lateral supports for creole use are inevitably greater . . . In area A [an area of relatively low Caribbean settlement] there were many black youngsters who knew and used very little creole [. . .] in Area B [an area with a higher density of Caribbeans] the use of creole was substantially greater amongst adolescents, and was also supported more strongly by continuities with the adult population (Hewitt 1986: 105)

There seems to be adequate reason to consider 'British Creole' to be a collection of local British varieties of JC, with some geographical differences. The research described in this book was carried out in London but it would be surprising if other communities of Caribbeans behaved in a completely different way, and much of the language behaviour reported by, for example, Sutcliffe and Edwards from elsewhere (Sutcliffe 1982a; Edwards 1986) is similar to that which I observed in London.

A role for Creole in education?

At the beginning of the 1990s the dynamism of British Creole as an oral form of language is not in doubt; its future in the home and in musical culture seems to be assured in the short term. We may reasonably ask now whether there is a role for Creole in more institutional domains as well. Has the time come for Creole to be used in education, for example? In the rest of this final chapter I will focus mainly on this question.

Early encounters

In keeping with the prevailing attitude towards New Commonwealth migrants, the initial attitude to the arrival of Creole in British schools was to see it as 'a problem'. The reaction of educators to Creole was confused by their view of it as simply 'substandard English': 'plantation English' in the words of a 1969 document published by the National Association of Schoolmasters (cited by Dalphinis 1991). This view, though transparently chauvinist and arguably racist in the British context, is not out of keeping with the view of Creole held at that time, and probably still widely held, by most people in the Caribbean. In spite of the recognition of the Creole 'problem', however, efforts to improve the situation were minimal until the publication of the Schools Council Concept 7–9 materials (1972). These materials themselves were problematic, though not all would go so far as Dalphinis and say that they 'were couched within the pathological framework which characterised much thinking on non-standard language at the time' (Dalphinis 1991: 53).

By the late 1970s most Caribbean children entering the school system were British born and were in close contact with peer groups of native British English speakers. Creole 'interference' with English no longer seemed to be such an important educational issue, although there continued to be confusion over the question of whether 'Creole-speaking' children were disadvantaged by virtue of their 'mother tongue', cf. Mungo 1979, who cites Caribbean research to claim that 'dialect does interfere to varying degrees in the acquisition of proficiency in the use of IAE (Internationally Acceptable English)' (Mungo 1979: 2). Meanwhile, Creole continued to be heard in British schools, giving rise to inquiries like that of Rosen and Burgess (1980) on the one hand, and on the other to defensive reactions from teachers and others in authority, who saw the use of Creole by those who they knew were capable of using British English as a deliberate challenge to the authority of the school.

Creole in the classroom?

By the early 1980s it was possible to discern two largely separate groups who favoured the introduction of some sort of Creole element in classroom work. On the one hand some teachers, in a spirit of multiculturalism and linguistic liberalism, sought to provide black pupils with a positive view of 'their own' language, by discussing its historical background and encouraging the use of Creole in creative writing. This approach had been advocated by Wight (one of the authors of the Concept 7–9 materials):

> The most effective way to guard against attacking the dialect is simply to place a positive value on it in class. Dialect differences can be considered objectively and older children can be encouraged sometimes to explore their own dialect and write in the style and manner of their [sic] culture. (Wight 1971: 5)

On the other hand, some parents, perhaps influenced by black consciousness ideology, wanted Creole to become a school subject. Probably both these groups were small minorities. However, their suggestions provoked a strong reaction from their respective majorities. 'Should I put Creole on the time-table? Over my dead body and the majority of my parents would cheer me to the skies. They want their children to get jobs,' wrote Max Morris, a London comprehensive school head teacher, to *The Sunday Times* (16.10.77) in a letter quoted by both Edwards (1979) and Stone (1981: 112). Stone's view is not all that distant from Morris's. She argues that

> Without saying that dialect should never be formally used in schools, I would argue that it is the job of the school to enable children to function with ease in the standard language. By the same token it is the job of the home, family and community to keep the dialect alive. (Stone 1981: 110)

Stone points out difficulties with an approach which involves the use of Creole language and literature in an attempt to enhance attitudes towards Caribbean culture and to promote a positive self-image among Caribbean pupils. She writes:

This approach ignores the historical fact that dialect has functioned as a source of self-esteem and the basis for an alternative value system from the times of slavery. It also assumes that the process of legitimization, through the acceptance of dialect for use in schools, is itself an enhancing process, which shows that the language is 'good' and has the teacher's approval. What it does not take into account is that the audience for this 'legitimization' may resist it, and react by modifying and adapting the original dialect, inventing new words in a continuing counter-action against absorption. (Stone 1981: 115)

However, while an attempt to 'legitimize' Creole may well produce a 'counter-action', it is fair to say that 'modifications' and 'adaptations' are taking place to Creole all the time, even in the absence of any 'legitimacy'. And such modifications and adaptations are a normal feature of Standard English as well – without making it any less standard or damaging its legitimacy, except from the point of view of purists.

Creole as Mother Tongue

Severe practical problems stand in the way of any attempt to introduce 'Creole' as a subject in its own right. Mother tongue teaching provision is a reality for ethnic minority children in many areas, supported by a mixture of state and minority-community funding (and sometimes funding from overseas governments as well): see Alladina and Edwards 1991: 20–25. It is safe to say that funds for this type of education are not ample, and this sort of 'minority-interest' area (as construed by Government and the dominant culture) is exactly the type likely to suffer in the prevailing climate of curriculum centralisation and public spending restraints and cuts.

The term 'mother tongue', is itself problematic when applied to Creole. Strictly speaking, there is a whole range of Caribbean Creoles which could be called the 'mother tongue' of the first generation who settled in Britain from the West Indies (see Chapter 2 and Appendix 1). If 'mother tongue' provision is what is required, then children of Jamaican parentage should learn JC, children of Dominican parentage Dominican, children of Guyanese parentage Guyanese, and so forth. In some cases, the numbers of speakers would be so small as to make it very difficult to argue for provision in particular districts and schools. Furthermore, there is a lack of the necessary back-up materials for teaching many of these Creole varieties: there are a few published reference works for JC, but none appropriate for school level work, while there is very little published about the other Creoles which could be of any use in classroom teaching. Major efforts would therefore be required to produce suitable materials and train teachers. This is by no means impossible, witness the success of the Patwa Project, an Adult Education project for St Lucian Kwéyòl speakers and learners, based in the London borough of Tower Hamlets (Nwenmely 1991); but the will must be present both on the part of funders and within the community itself.

There is also a problem of standardisation and spelling: there is no accepted written standard for any of the English-lexicon Caribbean Creoles used in Britain. The orthography of the *Dictionary of Jamaican English* (Cassidy and Le Page 1967, 1980) is excellent but virtually unknown outside academic circles. Other English-lexicon Creoles have no equivalent, though the *Dictionary of Jamaican English* system can be adapted to represent most of them. The French-lexicon Creoles are better off in this respect, having officially endorsed orthographies which, furthermore, are standardised among the different territories so that written St Lucian, for example, is essentially the same as written Guadeloupean Creole.

All of the above discussion overlooks the fact that from the point of view of black youth in Britain, there is only *one* Caribbean Creole variety which is significant among the peer group. This, I have argued in earlier chapters, is JC. Jamaican, while similar to the other English-lexicon Creoles, is not the 'mother-tongue', however defined, for a large proportion of the Caribbean population of Britain. Introducing JC as a subject makes more sense, in some respects, than introducing other Creoles, since the students' experience of it is likely to be more immediate. However, it could no longer strictly be called 'mother tongue' for most learners. A new set of arguments would be required to justify both its inclusion in the curriculum and the resourcing necessary.

'Language Awareness'

Some changes in the approach to English in English schools have provided Creole with other routes into the classroom. Limited use of Creole in written work was advocated e.g. by Wight (1971, see above) and later, for plays and creative writing, in the report of the Rampton Commission (Rampton 1981). An increasing interest in 'language awareness' in English lessons in the 1980s, and especially the emphasis on linguistic knowledge in the Kingman Report (1988), together with the introduction by some Examining Boards of new A-level examinations in English Language as an alternative to the existing English Literature A-levels, made it possible for teachers to include units on Creole as part of a wider study of 'language varieties' aimed at *all* pupils. A number of textbooks for use at GCSE or A-level have responded to this possibility. But the extent to which Creoles feature within 'language awareness' lessons, and the way in which the subject is treated, remains an unknown at this stage. Within the 'language awareness' framework, emphasis usually is placed on 'dialects' or varieties of English being different from, but not inferior to, Standard; and non-standard and Standard each being appropriate in different situations.[1] Thus a Caribbean child (who wrote that her parents spoke Creole at home, and outside the home as well 'I think') was able to write in class, in 1981, 'I feel that there is nothing wrong in speaking Creole as there is nothing wrong in speaking Cockney, but I feel that when you go for an interview or you are speaking to someone important you should try and speak as close as possible to Standard English.'

Teaching materials in this framework for Caribbean Creole are not plentiful, though the publication of the *Language and Power* materials by the ILEA Afro-Caribbean Language and Literacy Project (1990) has added substantially to the range available. The authors of those materials write that

Students' own knowledge and understanding of different languages and language varieties are an invaluable resource for language teaching. It is in this context that progress on the language issue in the multi-lingual classroom can be achieved, not just for students of Afro-Caribbean origin, but for students of all races and backgrounds (ILEA. 1990:v)

However, there is the possibility that teaching about Creole within the 'language awareness' framework runs the risk of perpetuating existing stereotypes: for example, Pardoe 1992, reviewing the *Language and Power* materials, writes: 'there is no reference to the Creole in Britain beyond music, literature, and creative writing, thus ignoring choice and switching in daily conversation and the (potential and actual) use of Creole in local business and services'. Teachers and authors need to pay careful attention to the contexts from which their materials are drawn.

Into the Future

Pardoe's remarks are a pointer to the future of British Creole: for, notwithstanding the publication from time to time of novels incorporating Creole dialogue (e.g. Simon 1982) or the fact that 'some very powerful Creole writing has emerged from British black schoolchildren, much of which is used as a regular classroom resource' (Dalphinis 1991: 54), it is as a spoken language in daily interactions, not just within the home but also, *in alternation with British English*, in many formal and informal encounters outside the home, that the future of British Creole lies. Paradoxically, the very 'illegitimacy' of the Creole seems to guarantee its survival for the time being: while other communities rally to protect their mother tongues from extinction in the face of the economic and cultural dominance of Standard English, British black Caribbeans preserve Creole on a day-to-day basis, without effort and, on the whole, without shame. That, at least, is the situation at the moment as I see it. Like all language situations, however, it is dynamic and these words will doubtless soon date. I hope that this book will at least serve to document the present dynamism of Creole in the mouths of young black Londoners.

Note

1. For further discussion and a critique of 'language awareness', see Fairclough, N. 1992. *Critical Language Awareness*. Harlow, Longman.

Appendix 1: The Two Systems

One aim of this book is to provide an insight into the main linguistic influences, whether Caribbean or British in origin, on members of the Caribbean community who were born in Britain. To do this it will be necessary to have, as 'reference points', descriptions of some sort of the grammar, phonology and lexicon of the languages concerned. In the best of all imaginable worlds, we would have clear-cut and non-confusing descriptions of all the languages in question – and a clear idea of exactly which languages those were. Unfortunately, it is in the nature of linguistic data to be fuzzy, fragmentary and sometimes puzzling. It is not clear what all the possible linguistic influences on young British Caribbeans might be, although the *main* ones are easy enough to guess at. Yet having guessed at what the relevant language varieties are, we do not have descriptions of exactly the form and detail that we would want. Inevitably, there will have to be compromises.

For reasons explained at the end of Chapter 1, this Appendix will concentrate on describing just *four* 'reference points' in order to help distinguish 'Caribbean' and 'British' linguistic influences in the language of my informants. The relevant varieties are: Standard British English (SBE), London English (LE), Jamaican Standard English (JSE) and Jamaican Creole (JC). There is particular emphasis on two of these, LE and JC. Reference will also be made to the written norm, here called 'Standard English' (SE).

Only those aspects of JC which are most relevant to the study of black English in Britain will be described here. The next few sections will provide a partial contrastive grammar of Caribbean

Creoles (principally Jamaican) on the one hand, and LE (with some references to SE/RP) on the other. For more information about the grammar and phonology of Caribbean Creoles, the following books may be helpful: Carrington 1984; Le Page and De Camp 1960; Cassidy 1961; Le Page 1961; Holm 1983, 1989; Le Page and Tabouret-Keller 1985. For further information on British English, the reader is referred to Milroy and Milroy (eds) 1993: *Real English: the Grammar of Non-standard English* (Longman, Harlow).

In this Appendix, each feature of grammar or phonology is identified by a letter (G = grammar, P = phonology) and a number in square brackets, thus: [P4], [G19]. These are used to refer to these features elsewhere in the text of the book.

Caribbean Creoles

There are already many descriptions of the grammar and phonology of Caribbean Creoles or Caribbean varieties of English. But while recognising the variability of the languages in question, nearly all of them choose to describe idealised abstractions from reality – a reality which, in view of the existence of the 'post-Creole continuum' (whatever the theoretical status of this label) – is quite complex. B.L. Bailey, for example, says (1971: 342): 'JC is . . . in my frame of reference, that form of language used in Jamaica which is syntactically, phonologically and lexically farthest removed from the Jamaican standard (SJE). It is the idealised construct which I described in *Jamaican Creole Syntax* (Bailey 1966).' Other linguists (e.g. D. Bickerton, C-J. N. Bailey) have focused on describing the 'continuum' itself, which makes their work difficult to use as a reference point for describing any single variety or 'lect'.

In describing the phonology of Caribbean Creoles, most writers have chosen to describe two discrete systems, 'standard' and 'creole', or 'acrolect' and 'basilect'. Wells (1982) for example, makes extensive use of these terms.

The following account of JC relies mainly on Bailey (1966) for the description of the grammar, and Wells (1982) for the description of the phonology. The orthography used in the grammar section is that used by Bailey, which follows Cassidy and Le Page (1980). The notation used in the phonology section is that of the source. [ ] indicates 'phonetic' transcription, and // indicates 'phonemic'.

London English

Perhaps ironically, the variety of British English that is most central to this study has not attracted so much scholarly attention. Accurate information on the grammar of LE is surprisingly hard to find: however, it appears that there are not all that many significant grammatical differences between LE and SE. Other British varieties like Geordie (Tyneside English) and Scots English differ much more from Standard. In the area of phonology, however, the differences between LE and Received Pronunciation are substantial. Fortunately there are a number of very good descriptions of London phonology on which I have been able to draw. Here, I shall rely mainly on Wells (1982).

The comparison: *Grammar*

(Note. Examples here are given in the transcription system of Cassidy and Le Page 1980, which is also used by most of the sources (e.g. B.L. Bailey 1966.) This differs from the system used for transcribing the conversational data elsewhere in this book, which uses an orthography based on Standard English.)

1. The pronominal system

SE has a pronominal system which marks a three-way distinction of person (first, second, third); singular and plural (except in second person, where *you* may be either singular or plural); and, in the third person singular only, gender (*he/she/it*).

[G1]: The 'basilectal' JC pronominal system lacks the gender distinction except for a distinction between 'common' and 'neuter' in third person, and has separate singular and plural forms in second person (cf. Bailey (1966): 22–4):

	singular	plural
1	mi	wi
2	yu	unu
3	im (*s/he*)	dem
	i (*it*)	

[G2]: Furthermore, SE pronouns are marked for case: thus a speaker must obligatorily (except in a few contexts) distinguish *I* from *me, him* or *her* from *he* or *she, they* from *them*. These distinctions are not part of the JC system, where *im* may translate *he* or *him* (or *she* or *her*), *wi* may translate *us*, and *dem* may translate *they* or *them*.

[G3]: SE also has a third set of personal pronouns, the possessives: *my, your, his, her, its, our, their*. These again are lacking in JC, where the simple pronoun from the set above may function as a possessive: *mi buk, yu buk, dem buk* etc: 'my book, your book, their book'.

Alternatively, JC uses the construction fi+pronoun: *fi-mi buk, fi-dem buk* etc.

The compactness of the Jamaican pronominal system as compared with that of SE reflects a more general principle of JC grammar: that nouns are invariant, taking no special forms to mark their grammatical roles.

LE is essentially the same as Standard with respect to the pronoun system.

2. Tense and aspect marking

The English verb can be said to have only two tenses: present and past. In the majority of verbs, past tense is marked with the suffix *-ed* or *-t*; but in a large minority of verbs, including many of the commonest, past tense is marked by a sound change: *sing – sang, leave – left, break – broke*. A few verbs have identical forms for both present and past: *hit, put*. There are some differences between SE and LE in this area: for example, the past tense of *come* and *give* in LE is the same as the present: *I come yesterday, I give him ten pence last week*.

Closely connected with the expression of tense in English is the category *aspect*. While verb tense refers to the absolute or relative time of an action, aspect refers to its completion or otherwise: *I am walking* (imperfective, i.e. non-complete) contrasts with *I have walked* (perfective, complete.)

Aspect in English is expressed by means of auxiliary verbs, especially *be* and *have*. There are also changes in the form of the verb itself involved in the expression of aspect: for example, the suffix *-ing* is required with *be*, and another form (the past participle, using ending in *-en/-ed/-t*, etc. is required with *have*).

The tense/aspect system of JC is fundamentally unlike that of English. The exact details are complex (and have been better studied for Guyanese than for Jamaican, see Bickerton 1973; Gibson 1982). However, there are obvious superficial differences in the way tense and aspect are marked. JC has two preverbal particles, *en* and *a*. Although these resemble (and may be derived from) the forms *are* and *been* of the English verb to be, *a* and *en* are not verbs. They are simply invariant particles, and cannot stand alone in the way that English *to be* can. Furthermore, their function is wholly different. Bailey (1966: 45–6) calls *en* a 'tense indicator' and *a* the 'aspect marker'. The following examples show the different tense and aspectual forms of the JC verb:

[G4]	(a) Mi ron	I run (habitually); I ran.
[G5]	(b) Mi a ron	I am running
[G6]	(c) Mi ena (en+a) ron	I was running
[G7]	(d) Mi en ron	I have run; I had run

For the purposes of comparing JC and British English, the most important difference lies in (a). The simple form of the JC verb, lacking either the tense or the aspect marking particle, may translate an English past tense. Bailey writes (1966: 45–6): 'If there is no tense indicator, the verb lacks time reference, and one must rely on the context for information.' She gives the example: *mi rait di leta yeside* 'I wrote the letter yesterday'.

The tense marker which Bailey cites as *en* does not usually appear in that form in British Creole. It occasionally appears as *bin*, a form which is also used in Jamaica. Much more frequently it appears as *did*, which seems to fulfil exactly the same function, and which also should be analysed as an invariant particle rather than a verb. The form of this particle is also subject to variation in the Caribbean region itself: for example, it has the form *ben* in St Vincent and *di* in Grenada (Le Page and Tabouret-Keller 1985: 89).

[G8]: While JC has no morphologically marked past tense forms corresponding to English (cf. looked, went, drove), in some cases the base form of the JC verb derives historically from an English past tense. Examples are *brok* (break/broke), *lef* (leave/left). These forms are used in JC for both present and past.

3. Plural Marking

[G9]: The category 'plural' is marked in English on most nouns, with the exception of personal names and nouns which refer to uncountable masses (e.g. gold, flour). JC does not mark the plural of nouns, except in the case of animate nouns, which may be followed by the affix -dem:

> di wuman-dem 'the women'
> di tiicha-dem 'the teachers'

4. Use of the copula

Both Standard and LE use the verb to be in the following ways (possibly among others):

(1) As an auxiliary verb: I am writing, etc.
(2) As an equative verb: I am a teacher, she is the doctor etc.
(3) As a locative verb: We are in London, I want to be here, etc.
(4) As a copular verb with an adjective: This book is old, I am tired now, they were fat, etc.

JC uses a different expression for each of these:

[G10]: (a) Auxiliary verbs are not used to form tenses or aspects of the verb in Jamaican, but the translation of SE sentences like these would require the JC particle *a*: *Mi a rait*, etc.

[G11]: (b) The JC equative verb is also *a* which 'regularly connects two nominals' (Bailey 1966: 32): *mi a di tiicha, im a di dakta*.

[G12]: (c) JC has a separate locative verb *de*: *Wi de a London, mi waant de ya*.

[G13]: (d) With true adjectives in JC, no copula is required. This can be explained by saying that in JC grammar, adjectives are a special class of verbs: they take the same preverbal tense/aspect marking particles as verbs. *Disya buk uold, mi taiad nou, dem bin fat*.

5. Negation

[G15]: The JC negator with fewest restrictions on where it may occur is *no*, as in: *mi naa (no+a) ron* 'I'm not running', *wi no de a London* 'We're not in London'. Other possible negators are *neba* or *neva*, used only for the past (*mi neba nuo dat*: I didn't know that) and *duont*, used for habitual action and with psychic state verbs (e.g. think) (Bailey 1966: 54).

Negation is one area where JC is in agreement with LE, and in contrast with the Standard. Both LE and JC require multiple negation in certain environments, although this does not occur in SE:

Im neva du notin	He never did nothing
Nobadi neva sii im	Nobody never saw him

6. Prepositions

[G16]: JC uses the preposition *a* where English would often use in, at or to.

Mi de a yaad	'I am in the yard' i.e., at home
Im de a skuul	'He is at school'
Im waant go a skuul	'He wants to go to school'

[G17]: Other JC prepositions may have an archaic flavour in modern SE: for example *pan* (from upon) which translates some instances of *on*.

[G18]: The English infinitive marker *to* is in most cases to be translated by *fi* in JC, although in some cases it is optional in Creole where it is obligatory in English (cf. *im waant go a skuul/im waant fi go a skuul*). In fact even in the Caribbean *fi* is considered to be a marker of extremely broad Creole; many otherwise broad Creole speakers will use *tu* (English to) in preference. (See Bailey 1966: 122ff for a description of the use of *fi*.)

[G19]: Question inversion. In formal and written SE questions, the auxiliary verb is 'inverted' or transposed around the subject of the sentence, e.g. *it was nice – was it nice*? Similarly with questions introduced by words such as *who* or *what*, unless these words are themselves the subject: who has he asked, what did she want, etc. In JC this process is totally absent (necessarily so with most verbs since tense/aspect are not marked by auxiliaries – see G4–G7.) Thus: *im bin a maakit*, 'S/he was at the market'; *im bin a maakit*? 'Was s/he at the market?' *we im a du*? 'What is s/he doing?'

Phonology

Excellent descriptions of Jamaican phonology – both of the Creole and Standard – already exist: for example, in the introduction to Cassidy and Le Page 1980, and in J. C. Wells 1982, 1973. There are also many other accounts, published and unpublished, of the phonological systems of other Caribbean Creoles. It would be superfluous for me to try to replicate them here. Instead, I will concentrate on pointing out the main points of contrast between Caribbean and British language varieties – just those which are most likely to be useful as a 'diagnostic' to decide which of those varieties we are looking at in a particular case.

J. C. Wells (1982) provides phonological descriptions not only of JC, but of the Standard and Creole varieties of several other Caribbean territories. From these descriptions it is apparent that the phonological differences between the different local standard varieties in the Caribbean are not great. Likewise the phonology of the Creole varieties is similar, though there are some differences, with the Western Caribbean varieties tending to cluster together and contrast with those of the Eastern Caribbean. In this section JC will be the basis for the contrastive description of 'Creole' and 'English', for reasons already given above. Occasionally I will refer to differences between Jamaican and other parts of the Caribbean.

In this section I will discuss only those elements of the sound system where there is at least a two-way contrast among the dimensions: JC, JSE, RP (Received Pronunciation), LE. While not wanting to rule out the possible influence of non-Jamaican accents from the Caribbean, or non-London accents of British English, I do not think these of sufficient relevance to draw them into the discussion at this point. Four dimensions of contrast will be enough for the time being. In fact there are not many points where the four systems show a four-way contrast; three-way contrasts and dichotomies are more common, with two or three of the varieties agreeing on a particular feature.

1. The vowels

I will follow the practice of phoneticians (e.g. J.C. Wells 1973, 1982) of using standard lexical sets to refer to groups of words containing a particular vowel. For example, by the LOT vowel I mean the vowel of the word *lot*, which in RP is approximately [ɒ], and in JC [a] (Wells 1982: 576). The LOT class consists of those words which share the vowel of *lot* in RP – *hot*, *shot*, *pot*; generally, these words will also rhyme with each other and with *lot* in Jamaican, although the sound of the vowel will be [a] and not [ɒ].

Table 1

Lexical set	JC	JE	RP	LE
[P1] HOT	a	ɒ	ɒ	ɒ
[P2] TRAP	a	a	æ	æ
[P3] STRUT	ɔ̈	ɔ̈	ʌ	ʌ
[P4] THOUGHT	a:	ɔ:	ɔ:	ɔ:
[P5] FACE	[iɛ]	[e:]	ɛɪ	[aɪ]
[P6] GOAT	[uɔ]	[o:]	əʊ	ʌʊ
[P7] PRICE	aɪ	aɪ	aɪ	ɑɪ
[P8] CHOICE	aɪ	ɔɪ	ɔɪ	ɔɪ
[P9] MOUTH	ɔʊ	ɔʊ	aʊ	æʊ~æ:
[P10] START	a:(r)	a:(r)	·a:	[ɑ:]
[P11] NORTH	a:(r)	ɔ:(r)	ɔ:	[ɒ ʊ]~ [ɒə]
[P12] FORCE	o:	o:r	ɔ:	o:
[P13] lettER ⎤	[ɐ],[ɔ̈ ɹ]	[ə]	[ə]	[ɐ]
[P14] commA ⎦				

Source: Wells 1982, vols. 2 and 3.

[P1–P3]: In the case of the short vowels, we find a contrast between Jamaican (both Creole and Standard) on the one hand, and British English on the other, except for the vowel of HOT, where the Jamaican acrolect has a sound similar to RP/LE. The vowel of STRUT in both JC and JE is described by Wells (1982) as 'back and rounded, between [ɔ] and [ɵ]' (p. 576).

[P4]. Likewise, JC is the 'odd one out' with the vowel of THOUGHT, which matches the vowel of BATH in JC, though not in any of the others.

[P5–P6]: The vowels of FACE and GOAT provide us with a possible four-way contrast. Describing Jamaican speech, Wells writes: '/e:/ and /o:/ are monophthongs in middle-class speech, but in popular speech usually falling diphthongs, [iɛ̈ ~ iɛ],[ʊɔ̈ ~ uɔ], thus face acrolectally [fe:s] and basilectally [fiɛs] . . .' (1982: 576). On the other hand, the LE and RP realisations of these diphthongs are also in contrast: LE /ʌɪ / vs RP /eɪ/. 'A London accent has an opener and more central first element, so that the diphthong ranges from popular London [ɛɪ] or [ʌɪ] . . . to broad Cockney [æɪ ~ aɫ]' (Wells 1982: 306). Similarly, the GOAT vowel shows a four-way contrast, with the typical LE realisations starting lower and further back than RP /əʊ/, and ending in a more central vowel. 'There is also a monophthongal variety, a frontish [ʌ:], reflected by eye-dialect spellings such as "nah" or "nuh" *no*' (Wells 1982: 308).

An additional complexity with the FACE and GOAT vowels is that in JC there is a small, closed set of lexical items which have these diphthongs in RP but have a short open vowel in JC. The most important ones are: *say, take, make* [sɛ tɛk mɛk], *go, so* [gɒ sɒ].

[P7–P8]: The vowels of PRICE and CHOICE have a similar realisation in JC, as /aɪ/, contrasting with the JE sound which is close to RP for both of these. LE, however, is different from RP with respect to these diphthongs: /ɑɪ/ as against RP /aɪ/ in price, while 'the starting-point of the CHOICE diphthong is characteristically rather closer in London speech than in RP: [ɔɪ ~ oɪ]' (Wells 1982: 308). Wells also mentions the possibility in London of pairs like *laugh* and *life* becoming homophones due to loss of the second element in the PRICE diphthong.

[P9]: MOUTH again provides a three-way contrast, with LE distinguished from RP. Discussing this at some length, Wells (1982: 309) mentions a number of LE or Cockney variants, the most stereotypical of them being [æ:]. In Jamaica and elsewhere in the Caribbean, there is a variant of this vowel found in words ending in /n/ or /n/ + consonant, e.g. round, town. These words may have the vowel of STRUT followed by /ŋ/, thus: [rɔ̃ŋ], [tɔ̃ŋ]. 'In Jamaica this pronunciation seems to be obsolescent, lexically restricted and avoided by educated speakers; but further south, in Trinidad and Guyana, it is much more generally to be heard, middle-class educated speech included' (Wells 1982: 572). It is certainly alive and well in London.

[P10–P12]: START and NORTH differ across the varieties in two dimensions: first, in vowel quality, and secondly, in the presence of /r/ following the vowel. The question of /r/ will be dealt with below. Meanwhile, note that the /r/-less Jamaican English pronunciations are similar to those of RP, but the LE pronunciations may be different. The vowel of START may be that of RP or it may have a 'fully back variant' (Wells 1982: 305), which according to Beaken (1971) characterises 'vigorous, informal' Cockney. The NORTH vowel is considerably closer in London speech than in RP, and is usually dipthongal. When it occurs in a closed syllable [sǫʊs] sauce – source, the diphthong is closing; but in an open syllable, it is centring: [lɔə], law – lore (Wells 1982: 571). The vowel of FORCE is different again: lacking /r/ in the basilectal Creole, its realisation in JE contrasts with LE on the dimension of rhoticity, while LE differs from RP in having a much closer vowel.

[P13–P14]: Finally, we have the quality of the unstressed vowel of the final syllable of lettER and comMA. Jamaican pronunciations of this vowel range from [ʊ] to [ə], with the possibility of /r/ where it occurs historically, as in *letter* (Wells 1982: 577). LE on the other hand may have 'very open realisations' of /ə/ (Wells 1982: 305), but these will never have /r/ even where it occurs historically, thus: [leʔʊ] letter. In British English and probably most other non-Creole varieties, the schwa ([ə] vowel) is a phenomenon associated with weakly stressed syllables. 'In West Indian vowels the most striking characteristic is the tendency to avoid central, [ə]-like qualities in favour of peripheral (unreduced) vowels. . . . The two syllables of matter rhyme: /ˈmata/' (Wells 1982: 571).

Consonants

There are relatively few differences between the Caribbean Creole and British English consonant systems but those there are seem to be very salient for speakers. There are also a few important differences between RP and LE. Only those which are significant for distinguishing 'Caribbean Creole' from 'British English' will be discussed here.

[P15]: Rhoticity. The historical /r/ in caRt, hoRse, letteR is well known to have been lost in the English dialects of South-East England, which are often called 'r-less'. This postvocalic /r/ is, however, a feature of many North American and Western British dialects, and in this case, Jamaican English patterns with them. Basilectal Creole also has /r/ postvocalically, 'except in weak syllables' or 'before a consonant in the same morpheme' (Wells 1982: 577); hence a contrast between JC /fa:m/ and JE /fa:rm/ 'farm'. In 'careful pronunciation of lettER words', according to Wells, 'mesolectal' speakers may pronounce /r/, though the usual unmonitored pronunciation of such words is r-less for all speakers.

The pronunciation of /r/ may be seen as a point of great variability for Jamaican speakers, especially those in Britain, since while the low-prestige varieties (JC and LE) agree in lacking rhoticity in many words, the high-prestige pronunciations (JE and RP) disagree on this feature.

[P16]: Postvocalic /l/. The /l/ of miLk and beLL is a point where there is a clear division between Jamaican on the one hand and British English on the other. Jamaican /l/ is invariably 'clear' in all contexts, i.e. pronounced with the tongue forward in the mouth. Both RP and LE have 'dark /l/' after a vowel, i.e. the tongue is retracted and the back of the tongue approaches the velum. Thus the /l/ sounds of *lip* and of *bottle* are different. However, LE takes the process a step further by vocalising /l/ in this context: it loses its character as a consonant and becomes a vowel, 'typically a close back vocoid of the type [o, ʊ]' (Wells 1982: 313). There is thus a very clear contrast between the JC/JE pronunciation of well [wɛl] and the LE pronunciation [wɛʊ].

[P17]: THink and boTHer. These consonants are the site of another three-way contrast. In JC, they are represented by the plosives /t/ and /d/: /tɪŋk/, /duo/. In JE they are /θ/ and /ð/ as in RP. In LE, a process called TH fronting may apply (Wells 1982: 328). The TH of *think* may be realised as /f/, while the TH of *bother* may be /v/, giving rise to two commonly cited examples of stereotyped Cockney pronunciation: 'fink' and 'bovver'. Word-initially as in THough, TH may be realised as 'any of [ðɪs, ðɪs, dɪs, lɪs, ʔɪs]' (Wells 1982: 329). JC and LE may thus agree on the pronunciation of this (as [dɪs]) while diverging dramatically on the pronunciation of think ([tɪŋk]/[fɪŋk]) and bother ([bada]/[bɒvə]).

[P18]: 'H-dropping'. The initial consonant of RP /hæt/ is subject to variation in many dialects of English. In RP, it is almost categorically present when it is present in the spelling. In other dialects, its distribution is more complicated. In LE, Wells notes

SE

(1982: 322) that 'pairs such as heat-eat, harm-arm' appear to be phonologically distinct, even if they are often phonetically identical'. Wells quotes Sivertsen (1960: 141): 'in really colloquial style its presence or absence cannot be considered contrastive; it may be missing in words where RP has it, and on the other hand it may occur where it is paralleled by no segment in RP, but never consistently one way or the other.' Furthermore, Sivertsen considers that [h] (which, it so happens, can only occur syllable-initially in English anyway) is to some extent a stylistic marker of emphasis, a feature it shares with [ʔ].

In Jamaica the situation is remarkably similar. 'Alongside the frequent H Dropping of [a:f] half, [uɔl] hole-whole, etc. there is the frequent use of [h] in words such as egg, off, end. This can be seen either as hypercorrection . . . or merely as an emphatic device used whenever a word beginning phonologically with a vowel is emphasised' (Wells 1982: 568). However, there is a geographical divide as well: in some rural western parts of Jamaica H Dropping is unknown 'and everyone, from top to bottom of the social scale, uses phonemic /h/' (Wells 1982: 569; see also Wells 1973: 12,93).

The fact that initial /h/ as an emphatic device is common to both JC and LE means it cannot be used for distinguishing between the two. However, it is interesting to note in the context of London that according to Hewitt (1986: 192) 'very emphatic initial glottal stops on words such as "'appen" and "'eart" are characteristic of creole-influenced LE'. The data discussed in this book contains examples of this, but there has been no systematic study of this phenomenon, or any attempt to make the notion of 'emphasis' explicit. It seems as though the glottal stop may have taken over the emphasis-marking role from /h/ in certain types of LE, but why this should be so is not clear.

[P19]: Glottalling. The glottalling of /t/ – replacing /t/ by a glottal stop as in [bʌʔə] butter is a central part of the Cockney stereotype. In fact, glottalling of other consonants is also very common in LE and is discussed at length by Wells (1982: 322–8). It seems that in the right contexts, [ʔ] may represent /p t k f v θ ð/: thus glottalling is rather a pervasive process in rapid informal Cockney speech. However, glottalling is *not* a feature of Jamaican speech at any level of society. Glottalling *is* known in the Caribbean, but only in Barbados: 'in the West Indies it is distinctively

Barbadian, and may be a local innovation' (Wells 1982: 584). Wells (1973: 31) notes a case of a 'West Indian' in London (presumably a Caribbean by birth) saying [boː? ə dɛm] both of them. This, he surmises, is the result of applying the London rule of /t/-glottalling to the Creole form [boːt] both. The resulting pronunciation is thus 'characteristic neither of West Indians in the West Indies nor of Cockneys in London, but just of West Indians in Cockney London'.

[P20]: Palatal and labial-velar glides. After /k/ and /g/ and before an open vowel, /j/ tends to appear in JC: /kjat/ cat, /kjaːr/ car, /gjal/ girl. The /j/ does not appear if the vowel corresponds to the classes LOT, THOUGHT, NORTH: this maintains the distinction between cot /kat/ and cat /kjat/. Similarly, /w/ may appear after /p b f v m/ before the vowels of NORTH, STRUT and CHOICE: /fwaːti/ forty, /bwai/ boy, /mwɒni/ money. /w/ before /ai/ occurs in words from the lexical set of CHOICE but not PRICE: hence /pwaint/ point but /paint/ pint. (See Wells 1982: 569.)

The foregoing has been an extremely brief and simplified description of the main points of contrast between SE and JC. It is not intended to be exhaustive: I have concentrated on those Creole forms which can best serve as markers of Creole when trying to distinguish a Caribbean Creole from a variety of British English. I have also concentrated on those forms which I know to occur in the speech of my informants: there are many other points of contrast which I have not discussed because they are not immediately relevant to the material in this book.

Appendix 2: The Conversations

The conversations from which extracts appear below were nearly all recorded by participants in the conversations using a portable tape recorder. When I was not present, whoever had custody of the tape recorder had complete control over what was recorded and passed on to me. In transcribing these conversations, I have therefore had to guess at the extralinguistic context in many cases. Recording and transcription of multi-party conversations presents many problems, and there are relatively few existing models for analysing this kind of data. Compromises have been necessary at several levels in order to arrive at a transcription which could be read without the sound being available. All transcriptions involve an element of interpretation, but these perhaps involve a little more than most: since in some cases it is not even clear *who* is speaking, and guesswork is needed.

In the interests of intervening as little as possible, only a simple portable cassette recorder was used, and no restrictions were put on where the participants should sit or how loudly they should talk. There were no radio or lapel microphones. The result is conversation which most of the time seems quite natural, with very few references to the fact that participants are being taped. The cost is that parts of the sound are lost due to poor recording quality, and much of the extralinguistic context cannot be recovered. In spite of these drawbacks (some of which might have been overcome with hindsight) I believe the method of letting informants make their own recordings has enabled me to collect better data than if I had been present on every occasion when a recording was made. The resulting data, although patchy and sometimes impossible to transcribe, at its best is very good.

A note on transcription

(See also the explanation of transcription conventions on p. ix.)

The conversation analytic approach taken in this book demands that the talk of each conversation be transcribed as accurately as possible, not only for the benefit of the analyst, but also for the benefit of the reader. Unfortunately, this is far from straightforward. It would be a naive linguist who thought that transcription of *any* sort could take place in a theoretical vacuum, and that merely by following a predetermined protocol one could arrive at *the* transcription of a given piece of talk. The problems – both practical and theoretical – which arise for the transcription of *monolingual* conversation are compounded when two or more languages are used in the same conversation. Further difficulties arise when one of these languages has no accepted orthographical system of its own, but is sufficiently similar to the other to be regarded as a (substandard) variant of it. This is the case in the present study, where in addition to (rare) instances of Standard English with near-RP pronunciation, we find conversations composed mainly of London English – grammatically close to Standard but phonologically different in several key respects – and Creole, which is significantly different from Standard at both levels.

One of the theoretical bases for the present book is that the reality of the two (or more) codes for the speakers cannot be simply taken for granted, but that the onus is on the analyst to demonstrate that participants in the talk *behave as if* there were two codes. This might argue for a system of transcription which is neutral between the two putative codes, for example using the International Phonetic Alphabet throughout. This, it might be argued, would least prejudice the reader in favour of the analyst's own conclusions, and would come closest to reproducing on the printed page the effect of hearing the original tape recording. I reject this proposal for two reasons: first, on the practical grounds that such a transcription would be difficult to read and would discourage many potential readers; secondly, on the more important theoretical grounds that 'phonetic script' in fact is *not* language-neutral, does *not* provide an equally accurate and impartial representation of the sounds of each variety, and would conceal rather than reveal the real judgements of the analyst – me – in respect of what he heard, which code it belonged to, etc.

A second alternative is available. Since the advent of Cassidy and Le Page's (1967, 1980) *Dictionary of Jamaican English* (DJE), there has been a published and accessible model of a phonemic orthography for Jamaican Creole. This orthography is excellent for representing Jamaican as well as other closely related varieties of Caribbean Creole, and has been used extensively by scholars, e.g. Bailey (1966), Sutcliffe (1982a), and of course Le Page. As an idealisation and abstraction away from the actual sounds of Creole it is at least no more, and at best considerably less distant, than ordinary English orthography is from the varieties of British English considered here. The convention of 'Standard orthography – British English: DJE orthography – Creole' has in fact been adopted elsewhere, e.g. by Sutcliffe (1982a), Sebba and Wootton (1984).

Difficulties arise, however, even with the above alternative. It is the very variability of the two codes in contact, and the subtle phonological cues which locate a particular item in one code or the other (for the analyst and perhaps also for the participants) which is a focus of interest in this study. Time and again I found myself being forced to make arbitrary judgements about how to spell words – by the Standard system, or by DJE? – when neither spelling seemed satisfactory by virtue of the sounds it seemed to represent. How, for example, should one write the word [fru:] in the mainly Creole sentence [yu: na go ron fru: dis djam brık wa:l] ('you're not going to run through this damn brick wall')? DJE spelling dictates *tru*, which obscures just what is most interesting about the word – the fact that it shows TH-fronting (/θ/ → /f/) 'as if' it were the British English word 'through' given its working-class London pronunciation. To use the Standard orthography *through* would equally deprive the reader of that information, while at the same time making a new *theoretical* claim: that the word in question involves a 'switch' from Creole to Standard, for that word only. The 'eye dialect' spelling *frough* (though it may strike the reader as strange) has the advantage of drawing attention to the first consonant of the word, but makes the same questionable theoretical claim as *through*.

An additional complication is that many words in the London Creole vocabulary – for example, many which belong to what Hewitt calls the 'multiracial vernacular' – are strongly identified with 'Black' culture but are historically words of British English. Should I then write 'dread' as *dread*, claiming it for British English, or *dred*, assigning it to Creole? Similarly 'wicked', 'Blues', 'sound,' and so on.

In the end I have chosen a solution which addresses some, but not all of the problems. I have used an 'eye-dialect' style of transcription which roughly represents the phonology of both London English and Creole, and gives a guide to the actual sound when taken in conjunction with the directive that underlined stretches are 'pronounced as if Creole'. Within the transcription, certain differences from Standard orthography are used systematically to show pronunciations characteristic of one or other variety. Thus an apostrophe indicates a 'missing letter' (*not* a 'missing sound'): *not'in'* for 'nothing' pronounced as [notn], where a true 'eye-dialect' spelling might be *nutt'n* or the like. This is done on the assumption that readers used to Standard orthography will have no trouble recognising the word by what remains of it, plus the knowledge of where in the word the missing letters occur. Where appropriate, *d, f* and *v* are substituted for *th*, thus *dem, frough*, etc. Problems remain: how to represent 'other'? For the Creole pronunciation *oder* looks odd (but no less recognisable than JCE *oda*) but for London English, *over* has the disadvantage of already existing as a Standard English spelling for another word, while *uvver* is a fairly standard eye-dialect spelling but is unsystematic and perhaps counter-intuitive for those unfamiliar with this variety. In cases like this the best solution seems to be to use the standard orthography, and put the IPA transcription in brackets.

One convention observed throughout the transcriptions is to use '%' to represent orthographic *t* which is pronounced as a glottal stop. This 't-glottalling' is characteristic of London and other British varieties but is not normal in the Caribbean outside Barbados; thus it is of particular interest and is marked throughout. Thus *par%y* 'party' and *bu%* 'but'.

Underlined sections of text are to be taken as representing, in the view of the analyst, stretches of talk which can be identified – mainly on phonological grounds but with allowances also for grammar and morphology – as 'Creole' in contrast to British

English. Consonants and vowels in these stretches are thus to be 'read' as having their Creole values. Where particular non-Creole features occur embedded in these stretches they will be pointed out, where relevant, in the commentary.

The best that the transcription presented here can hope to achieve is to provide an easy-to-follow record of the conversation with an indication of how each utterance sounded; and in addition to avoid a covert theorising of which code an item belongs to. No doubt some readers will not be happy with this transcription system, but I hope it will suffice for the purposes of this book.

Conversations A, B, C

These conversations took place in a family home in East London. Two generations of the family lived together in the house, but of the younger generation, some were Jamaican-born and others, like Brenda, were born in Britain. Brenda, then aged about eighteen, was my main informant and had custody of the tape recorder. Brenda's father, aged about fifty, was born in St Mary's, Jamaica: he is a retail worker. His brother Robert, and Brenda's brother Lenny, are both also Jamaican by birth. The three men all speak with more or less strong Jamaican accents. Brenda's father's speech is generally closest to Standard but his pronunciation has a few London English features, while there is clear Creole influence on his grammar. Robert has a very marked Jamaican accent and some Creole grammar features. Lenny, who is a Rastafarian, often uses a style close to basilectal Creole and his pronunciation is strongly Creole.

Conversation A: *Setting the world to rights*

B: Brenda
F: Brenda's father
L: Lenny
R: Robert

(A-1)

```
1→ B   it's only because there's halfcastes in it now, right
       ┌ why (0.4) there's a mixup
    F  └ no no no, I'm not talkin' I'm not ┌ sayin'
    L                                      └ no no
```

```
 5        me a show you (we as a) race (Brenda),
          is a example me a show you right *⎡ * * all the
          races should come together right  ⎢
     B                                       ⎣ if there wasn't no
 →        halfcastes then you could distinguish, right
10   ?F    ⎡ distinguish
     B     ⎣ cause some of them you see, (.) outside the street, (.)
 →        right, ⎡ and you say da% is a halfcaste
     ?L          ⎣ an' you don' know you can't * *
 →   B    ⎡ an im stone black he he you know what I mean?
15   F    ⎣ e:::: yeah yeah
 →   B    stone black
     (0.6)
     ?L    (cause) I ⎡ know * true
     F                ⎣ no sir no sir
20   B    yes daddy, oh come off it, there's (Holly)
     R    * generation * it's a whole generation
          you no ⎡ see it
     F           ⎣ (yes a can't be full black)
     L    it's a way it's a way ⎡ (0.4) how do you t'ink seh,
25   B                          ⎣ whe you mean?
     L    how do you know what you is, dat's what me
          was comin' to (0.6) seh (.) you know wha' I mean?
          ⎡ when you say (he's a)
 →   B    ⎣ (well) I mean by stone black I mean their
30        parents ⎡ is
     L            ⎣ how do you know what you is
```

(A-2) [Later in the same discussion]

```
 1   F    nobody have the money (1.0) the kids gets the money (1.0)
          and he just free to say I'm going to hold onto this type of
          money / and no powers on de hearth take // it away from me
          again
     B    I always say, right
 5   L    * * that's it, that's it
     B    I always say, right,
     (0.4)
     F    and he know he can't finish it too
 →   B    daddy PLEASE!
10   ?    (yeh) he know ⎡ too
 →   B                  ⎣ I always say, right, if at first you poor [pʊəɹ],
          right, an' den you get rich, when you lose it all you no feel no
          way cause you know you can still ru:n
```

```
        ?R   no (.) (you get) * * *
   15   F  ⎡ no, no, no, no
        L  ⎣ but / (den) but / (you do need some) you do you don' 'ave
        B    yeh
        B    yes
        B    I'm not (.) but there again, you can still survive / (0.4)
   20→       because you know what it's like to be poor [pʰɔə]// (0.8) ///
             right? but a rich for a rich for for a rich person to lose all
             their money right and to become poor [pʰɔə] that's a hard
             fing that's a heartbreak tha% is
        R    yes
   25   R    yes
        L    yes but you don't
        L    (still) (still) fallin' from one state, right, fallin' from rich:
             (0.8) to poor / is two different – is two different – is two
             different way right
   30   B  ⎡ dat is two
        F  ⎣ is two different ways
        B    I know
```

(A–3) [Later in the same discussion]

```
    1   L    (so) them they call wicked people, right (0.4) (think of) people
             will do, people (0.8) many other t'ings right / (0.4) and becau'
             society don't like dem t'ings dere in first place, right, (0.4)
             you know wha' I mean, dem hafi be lock (0.8) (up)
    5   B    m::
        L  ⎡ because society (don't want them in it)
    →   B  ⎣ because, because them start / it off in first place dey know
             it's wrong (.)
        ?    right dem (no really)
   10   B    so dey know 'ow to (1.0) put ⎡ a stop to it
        F                                 ⎣ yeh but I say what I'm saying, it
             shouldn't be so ⎡ that's what I'm saying, it shouldn't be so
    →   B                    ⎣ it shouldn't be so, but it is so
```

Conversation B *The right kind of guy*

All the participants in this conversation are of Brenda's own
generation. Jane, her cousin, is also British-born. Trevor is a
friend of Brenda's brother Lenny.

(B–1)

    B   I wanna guy (0.4) my guy (.) ('as) – I've gotta see that guy (.)
        'e mus' 'ave ambition, (0.2) I must see that me 'n 'im can
        work togevver, right an' – (1.0) build fings (0.6) / (0.2) build
        fings togevver you know what I mean // I wanna know say,
        this guy is an impen – independent guy /// who can do fings on
→   'is own, I can't find I can't find all that <u>shi%%eries in a day</u>!
                                            <"shitteries" = junk, nonsense>
    ?   yeah
    ?   yeah
    ?   yeah
    ?   yeah
  (1.0)
    J   you can't
    ?   no you can't
    J   you can't know one man in (.) I tell you s- (it) sometimes it
        takes years

(B–2)

1   B   'ang on a minute * I'll tell you now⌈ * (anybody)
    ?   ⌊ it's wrong though
    B   goes to me, right, go outside for (me) freshair I don't
        wanna go outside for fresh air, right, <u>me na go outside</u>
5   ⌈ <u>for no fresh air</u>
    J ⌊ even if you do go out for fresh air it don't mean you're
        gonna have sex outside there
    L   <u>hey it hot in 'ere you know Jane you wan' come outside ya</u>
    J   * *
10   < all laugh>

(B–3)

1   B ⌈ but 'e wouldn't be there!
    T ⌊ (you needn't leave 'is room) (.) you needn' leave 'is room
    B   'e wouldn't / even be around (0.6) ⌈ when <u>I</u> a sleep
    ?S yeah!
5   T   ⌊ (you needn't even) leave 'is
        room
  (1.O)
    B ⌈ <u>'im hafi broke inna my house</u>
    T ⌊ * * * * * * * 'is car, even if 'e's in 'is car, man

10→ B I wouldn't sleep in 'is car ⌈ me na sleep in 'is car for me have
    ?   ⌊ (see these people)
    B me bed at home
    ? ooh, ⌈ god
    T   ⌊ * there's a lo% of things might 'appen
    B no, I don't business, no:!

(B–4)

1 J when we was in the hall:
   (0.2)
   ? ⌈ ah yeh yeh
   ? ⌊ * * * yeh yeh
5 B now 'e ad everyfing if you was to sit down an
      'ear that guy speak (.) ⌈ 'e (was going) to Jamaica
                              ⌊ 'e was ni:ce (0.8) 'e was ni:ce
   B 'e was going to build 'is place (0.6)
      ⌈ 'im a build 'is business (1.0)
10 ? ⌊ ye:h 'e was NI:CE man
   B an' it's the type of guy like that (0.6) I ⌈ want
   ?   ⌊ yeah
   (0.6)
   B ⌈ know what I mean? But there again, those things didn't even
15 ? ⌊ * * * * * * * * * * * * *
   B ⌈ enter my mind turaatid!
   ? ⌊ * * * * * *

(B–5)

1 J if the guy will come up to you and say 'I hear say you want me'
      (0.4) / he must've got the impression that you were running you
      were [mock panting] 'oh (you) (god) 'e's nice yeah, I wan' 'im //
      ***' you know that shi%%ries?
5 ? YEAH
   ? YEAH
   ? that's the ⌈ sort of (pushy man) * *
   B   ⌊ (so) I had to say 'did I really? (0.6) I
      ⌈ did I really?'
10 J ⌊ yeah (.) and that is the right way to be
   (0.8)
   ? mmm
   (J) ⌈ * * * *
   B ⌊ then I just laughed (0.6) and then 'e – 'e just pulled me for a

15   dance – I didn't mind dancin' wiv 'im / 'cause <u>me know say,</u>
        <u>me no 'ave nothin' inna my mind</u> // but to dance, and then
        we star%ed to talk and all the rest of it /// and tha%'s it ////
        <u>full stop!</u>
        J   yeah
20   J   yeah
        J   yeah
        J   yeah
    (2.0)
        J   'e was a nice guy, but differently, right

Conversation C: *The Domino Game*

These conversations took place in the course of a domino game
played by Lenny and some male friends (M and N). Brenda was
present though from the tape it is not clear whether or not she
was actually playing. The words 'fire', 'telephone', 'pin', 'needle'
and 'crablouse' appear to be code words which are used to communicate by partners who cannot see each other's tiles. Much of
this tape was indistinct because of the noise of dominos crashing
on the table!

(C–1)

 1   M   <u>telephone</u>
     (2.0)
        N   * * * <u>fire</u>
        B   <u>fire</u> ⌈ (wid) telephone FIRE < laughs>
 5   N   ⌊ Michael you * * * *
        < laughter>
        B   <u>Where you get all them (thin) word from</u>
     (2.0)
→   B   What does telephone ⌈ mean please?
10   ?   ⌊ (mix)
     (1.2)
        B   What does telephone mean?
        M   * * man * * (I've got no chance) * *
        B   Come <u>strong</u> kleenex e <u>ha ha ha ha</u> ⌈ ha
15   N   ⌊ (jus') gedoff!
        B   sorry! ('im t'ink) < laughing>
        M   how much you have sir?
        B   <u>him tryina con-concentrate</u>

```
         N    * * *
   20  (0.5)
         B    concentration! a ha con.cen.trate
         N    ah no ah no ah no ah no ah no
        (0.5)
   25  M    you pass?
```

(C–2)

```
    1  L    who ena get off course?
       B    'ear 'im now no! he he
            (you) slap down
            'im say / 'pin' // (0.8) 'im slap down 'im say 'needle' ///
    5       'im slap down i what did you say again? (0.6) ///
            (0.8) what did you say?
       M    (pin)
       M    ha ha ha
       M    ha ha ha
   10  M    eh ha ha ha
     ?L    crablouse
       B    ehe crablouse  ⎡ i:s
                           ⎣ hi hi hi hi

            ha ha
   15  B    juk
            < 'juk' = 'poke', usually obscene>
```

(C–3)

```
    1  M    you wan% a swee%ie?
       (2.8)
       N    you got ONE?
       M    m:hm (.) one that (you suck)
    5  (5.0)
       B    can I have sixty please?
       M    me na sell sweet now y'know (0.5) you want buy quar%ers
       N    hahaha (.) blodklaat!  ⎡ if you give 'em free Brenda wouldn't
       B                           ⎣ him want one (for eat)
    9  M    want it hahaha
   10  M    you (want) buy quarter then? he he he
       N    that's what I was doin'
        ?    ⎡ huh?
       B    ⎣ him want eat you up * * * (him pitch devils)
   15  ?N   he he he
```

Conversations D, E and F

Conversations D, E and F took place in a flat in South-East London. The main participants are young and British-born: Valerie (twenty-two), Colette (seventeen), Laverne (seventeen), (Valerie's cousin), Natasha, a little girl, and a baby. Valerie's Caribbean-born mother participates in conversation E. Valerie, Colette and Laverne do not have noticeable Jamaican accents when speaking 'ordinary' English, and only Laverne uses Creole syntax, once, *without* Jamaican pronunciation.

Conversation D: *The Photo Album*

In this conversation, Valerie, Colette and Laverne are looking at photographs taken some months earlier.

(D–1)

```
 1   C    that's a picture of me when we had nothing to do (3.6)
     V    so who's this? (1.0) ⌈ These two
     C                         ⌊ They were some people at the party
    (2.2)
 5   V    what's their names?
    (0.4)
     C    I don't know you'll have to ask Valerie
     L    Valerie (.) who? Who are these?
    (3.0)
10   C    who are they?
     V    some girl who used to go to my school Jackie and I don't
          know who that is / somebody's
          em
    (0.2)
15   C    is that her man
     V    uh-m (.) Somebody else's man.
     C    o::h.
     L    (Is that my nice sweet *)
     V    (So) them a hogop!
20   < laughter (1.4)>
     ?    ⌈ you hear it?
     ?    ⌊ [ oh dear
     V    that's what he took one of me like that as well
          I had to hide it you know / I had to hide it // I had to hide it
```

25   from Ricky I couldn't show Ricky when I said to Ricky look
        (0.2) some guy took a photograph of me huggin' up
        < 'ignorant' voice>
        'Duh! (.) You shouldn't let no man hug you'
     baby NA:ME:DE:
     C   shut up Courtney
30   L   it's true
     (0.6)
     L   aah! Colette < laughter (1.2)>
     C   no Laverne (0.1) Laverne you shouldn't take no more pictures
         like that of me
35   L   no, sorry right you didn't want me to take [tɛk] it over
         you right I just had to sneakup
     V   <u>You see (wha woman wear no)</u>
         < laughter (0.5)>
     C   what was I ⌈ wearin'? that's Nicolette!
40   V   ⌊ *   *   *   *   *   *   yeh look at her in her
         (sexy) jean guy (.) deadly!
     ?   <u>e͢h h͢e͢h</u>
     C   'n 'er trousers
45   L   hih that's me! (0.6) ⌈ <u>Valerie cut me off there</u> <u>bwo::y</u>!
     C   ⌊ (must be the one in my bathroom)
     V   no I never! It's just my wardrobe that's all
     (1.0)
     C   half of the pictures you just see ⌈ one little corner
50   ?V   ⌊ you know what I mean!
     < laughter (1.4)>
     (2.0)
     V   (but listen now) when I show anybody this they
         say '<u>watch she pose n</u> ⌈ <u>ow</u>!'
55   ⌊ < laughter (4.0)>
     (3.0)
     V   that's that's Colette my friend's (1.0) sister
         that's her man the one that was huggin' me up there
         ⌈ with that uvver gal
60   ?L ⌊ o::::h!
     (1.0)
     L   <u>(watch she a pose dere)</u>
     (0.6)
     ?   e-eh!
65   ?   m-hm

(D–2)

```
 1   V   who's this
        (0.5)
         L   that's at (1.0) that's  ⌈ at 'er party
                                     ⌊ oh yes
 5  (2.5)
         V   wh ⌈ at was it for?
        ?C     ⌊ (you can hardly see Laverne)
         V   I was DJ, yeh you know I chopped her ⌈ off ***
                                                  ⌊ < laughter>
10  (2.0)
         L   you should see out the camera
         V   I did I did see it good
         L   did you
         V   yeh but I must have moved innit
15   C   Laverne's clothes look bigger now Laverne * * *
         V   you what? (0.8) her clothes < laughter (3.5)>
        (2.0)
         V   Just hangin' innit
        (3.0)
20   V   'how should I pose?' she's goin' to me
             I said 'pose anyhow'
         ?   eh he he
         V   'is this alright?'=
25   = < laughter>
         C   your one come out good Viv
```

(D–3)

```
 1   V   oh it's a laugh is that one (0.8) watch * *
             watch she a skyank!
         < laughter (3.0)>
         V   did (did you leave) the radio on *? was the radio on?
 5   ?   yeh
         C   were you dancin' Laverne?
         L   yeah man, see the grooves man
         C   I thought you was kissin' at the camera or somep'n, I don't
             know what ⌈ you were doin'
10   L              ⌊ it looks as if I was runnin' out the door!
         < laughter (1.5>
         ?   (you cocky kick at you lick though) innit
         < laughter (2.0)>
```

(D–4)

```
 1   V   that's my mum.
         < laughter (2.5)>
     C   that's the old fashioned style ⎡ right
     L                                   ⎣ what's she doin' cleanin the
 5       house
     V   I said to her (1.0) come and take a photograph
         'Who me? you mad! Inna dis kinda state?'
   (0.8) hhh < laughter (2.0)>
     V   I said to her 'pose anyhow' (1.5) ⎡ She says 'is dis alright?'
10                                          ⎣ yeh
     C   (Put 'em) on television heh heh
```

(D–5)

```
 1       were you dancin' Viv
         yeah, skankin' innit
         m-hm
         wh-what music was on?
 5       can't remember most probably Dennis Brown or something
     V   like that any more, is there any old ones in there?
     ?   ⎡ nah::
     C   ⎣ no just this wicked one of Laverne innit he he
 9   V   where's that one of me that was huggin' up that guy have you
         got it there in your house?
     L   you hid that me no know where you put it
         [Note: no Creole pronunciation]
     V   where did I put 'em ⎡ (what if)
15   ?                       ⎣ I don't know * * Ricky ⎡ * *
     V                                                ⎣ I'm sure
         I gave them to you Laverne
     L   you never give it to me (1.5) You only give me me nursery
         ones
```

(D–6)

```
 1   L   oh that's one of me: (.) in me shorts
     V   oh ⎡ ri:ght!
     C      ⎣ * * (off her chin)
         she's trying to blow a model here me no know
 5 (2.2)
```

```
    L   Courtney (2.0)  < popping> sound uh-u ⎡ h::!
                                              ⎣ < laughter>
   (2.5)
    L   uh-uh:::  < laughter> and silence (4.0)>
    C   Andrea (2.0) ⎡ say Andrea (1.5) Courtney say Andrea
                     ⎣ mhm
10 (2.0)
    C   ⎡ go on
    C   ⎣ Andrea! (2.0) Andrea! ⎡ (2.5) Andrea! ⎡ (3.0) Nyeah!
    ba                          ⎣ uhuh          ⎣ uhuh nyee
   (2.0)
15  C   dribble dribble (4.0) dribble dribble
   (2.0)
    V   (you see him play wid) di bubble  ⎡ dem!
                                          ⎣ < laughter (2.0)>
   (3.0)
    V   blow the bubbles Courtney
20  ba   a:: nye
    V   Courtney, blow the bubbles
   (5.0)
    V   Courtney, look how ya aunty do ya hair and look how it stay
        now!=
    = < laughter (1.5)>
25  V   watch a 'souly' look now, alright!
```

Conversation E: *Who'll do the dishes?*

Participants in this conversation: Valerie, Laverne, Valerie's mother, Natasha, a child of about four. Natasha speaks with a London accent. All Valerie's mother's utterances have a strong Caribbean accent.

(E–1)

```
1   V   c'mere a minute (1.2) Tasha: < laughter> 'old on,
        stay there I 'aven't finished you yet
    N   < giggle> awright
    V   (bet you) not washin' up the dishes
5      (0.2)
    L   nor me! I'm goin' over to the park anyway t-
    M   unu better go wash up di dishes!
    L   eh heh he he no: I was gonna take he he I'm gonna take, um,
        Natasha over the park / there
10  M   o:h!
```

(E–2)

1	M	Laverne <u>a your turn</u> to wash up the dishes
→	L	I said <u>me na a do it</u> ((giggle))
	M	<u>you a joke man</u>/ (0.8) come on man (you no) / <u>finish</u>
		<u>wi' what you doin'</u> (there) an wash the dishes come on man
5	(L)	< laughs> Na(ʜʜ)aew
?		* *
	V	you can't draw Laverne what'd you say your drawring
	L	I'm drawing Tasha
	N	why don't YOU go wash the plates up
10	M	<u>I wash it up dis mornin'</u>
		(0.8)
	N	⌈ (still go washed up)
	V	⌊ I washed it up yesterday (0.8) do you wanna wash them, Tash?
	N	No (0.4) I can't wash
15		(0.8)
	V	why?
		(1.6)
	M	<u>make breakfast, dinner, wash up plate, no man (no can do,</u>
		<u>little more some)</u>
20	V	we 'elped
	M	m: m: (<u>woman drop it</u>)
	V	didn't we 'elp, Laverne
	L	yuh: (0.4) well, Valerie should wash it I reckon * *
		(0.4)
25	V	look at yeh yeh yeh yeh yeh yeh you left your <u>dutty clothes down</u>
		<u>'ere</u> an' um innit, mum? an we wa – <u>an' we wash de</u> clothes
		for you?
		(1.0)
	L	didn't ask you to
		(0.6)
30	V	innit mum?
		(0.8)
	M	<u>me na say a word</u>
		< all laugh>
	M	< laughs> <u>tape over thereso</u> (0.8) <u>that damn tape there you see</u>
35		< laughter (5.0)>

(E–3)

1	V	where's the knife mum?
		(2.4)

```
    M  Lord (munumun) look fe someting man! Cha (1.0)
       where's a dis where's a that (1.2) find it unu self man
 5  V  ih hi hi hi
   (1.2)
    M  uh huh
    V  all right, there's no need to shout
    M  let the man have a good laugh ha ha
```

Conversation F: *Where's my mini?*

Valerie and Laverne. Laverne shouts to Valerie who appears to be in another room.

(F–1)

```
 1  L  where's my mini?
   (0.4)
    V  wha% mini? (2.2)
    L  see you (say you) don't know no mini the ** mini that I wore
 5     there (* * drink * *)
   (8.0)
    L  (get murder) guy!
→   V  I do:nt knoh where it is! (1.4) see it there?
    L  caught you (frown) didn't I?
10  V  ha ha ha ha ha hi hi hi ha::: < laughter (4.6)>
   (3.4)
    V  ah?
    L  (shi:t) Valerie!
15→ V  What? Whe you a call me name for
   (0.4)
    L  Look in the wardrobe to see whether you see it
    V  see wha:'
   (0.4)
20  L  ME MINI:! ⎡ please
    V            ⎣ yer mini yer mini (0.2) twix' yer legs
    L  yeah * *
```

Conversations G and H

These conversations are all different from the preceding ones in that the recordings were made in schools rather than family homes, and the participants were left alone in the room with a large portable reel-to-reel tape recorder and asked to have a conversation. As the participants were aware that they were taking part in research focused on language, and 'black' language in particular, and as the setting was rather an odd one for a friendly chat, the resulting language behaviour can be taken as unnatural to that extent. The following extracts, however, show behaviour that seems natural enough, and is comparable with other linguistic behaviour recorded in a more normal setting.

Conversation G

Jane and Cheryl, two girls from Catford: Jane aged 16, Cheryl aged 15. Jane's parents are both from Kingston, Jamaica and Cheryl's from St Ann's, Jamaica.

```
1   J   * * * she never did invite me (0.2)
        are YOU goin'
    C   no she never invite me neither
    J   's not fair
5   C   no, she invite (0.4) um (.) you know Johnny ?
    J   yeah
    C   him tell me (0.8) and my mum went to her house and she
        said (0.4) she's o- she just told 'er she's 'avin' a christenin'
        (0.2) me no know if me a go
10  (0.4)
    J   so how old is the baby then?
    (0.4)
```

Conversation H

B is Brenda, of conversations A–C; this recording was made when she was aged about seventeen, still in the sixth form. A is a friend of St Vincentian/Trinidadian parentage. Recorded in a school in East London.

(H–1)

```
1   B   anyway Amy (.) ⎡ choh (0.8) Karen tol' me (.) (yes)
    A              ⎣ Karen
    B   this is Karen to me now (0.4) she goes to me (0.4) well (0.8)
        about I mus' come to 'er par%y right,
    A   ⎡ 'cause she told you, innit?
    B   ⎣ yeah mhm:: ('course 'n' that) (0.2) yeah
    (0.4)
```

B   right well anyway I went down there / (1.0) <u>me bring my</u>
      <u>sister-dem a:ll me sister-dem come wid me y'know</u> (0.9) //
      <u>come all the way down the</u> (.) ah (.) /// party there
      she <u>goes</u> to me abou% (i%) <u>now when we ge% there</u> (0.2)
      <u>we walk pas'</u> the door (to) <u>number fifty- nine – no lights!</u>
A   mhm
A   m:hm
A   party
A   mhm:
(0.4)
B   righ%, (0.6) so (w') walk up the top of the road: (0.2) couldn't
      'ear no music at all so <u>my sister-dem start cussin' me like any-</u>
      <u>thing you know</u> (.) 'bout me bomboklaat ⌈ <u>an' all dis business</u>
A   ⌊ n:hhhn
      dere (0.2) <u>well anyway</u> (0.4) <u>go back down dere,</u> right (0.6)
      <u>an' we look ('pon *) now we see</u> (0.6) Jerry (but dem) <u>come</u>
      <u>tell us</u> ⌈ 'bout um, aks us where de ⌈ party de (0.6) right?
A   ⌊ m::   ⌊ party is
B   so <u>we say</u> well definitely <u>we come up</u> 'ere cause
      Karen say it was 'ere, right?
A   yeah
B   couldn' fin' <u>not'in'</u> so (0.4) we wen% <u>back down dere</u>
      <u>lookin' at de gates</u> (0.8) / <u>we find a letter thereso</u>
      <u>f' say 'bout</u> (0.2) <u>party cancel</u>
A: m::

(H–2)

1   B   Na:h (0.6) (up) (0.4) Tuesday 'e told
           whasisname (t) <u>come – come phone me</u> right (0.2) <u>So me me –</u>
→   (0.8) what 'appened u:m (0.2) yeah,
           so I phone <u>Winston</u> and tell Win- and tell Winston
5   (and) 'e goes to me 'e wants to go out (0.6)

Bibliography

Adelman C 1976 The language of teenage groups. In Rogers S (ed) *They Don't Speak Our Language*. London, Edward Arnold, pp. 80–105.

Alexander Z, Dewjee A 1981 *Roots in Britain*. Brent Library Service.

Alladina S, Edwards V (eds) 1991 *Multilingualism in the British Isles, Volume 2: Africa, the Middle East and Asia*. Harlow, Longman.

Alleyne M 1980 *Comparative Afro-American*. Ann Arbor, Karoma Press.

Anderson B 1983 *Imagined Communities. Reflections on the Origin and Spread of Nationalism*. (Revised and extended edition 1991) London, Verso.

Atkinson M, Heritage J 1984 *Structures of Social Action: Studies in Conversation Analysis*. Cambridge, Cambridge University Press.

Auer J C P 1981 *Bilingualism as a Members' Concept: Language Choice and Language Alternation in their Relation to Lay Assessments of Competence*. Papiere des Sonderforschungbereichs 99, Konstanz No. 54.

Auer J C P 1984a *Bilingual Conversation*. Amsterdam/Philadelphia, John Benjamins.

Auer J C P 1984b On the meaning of conversational code switching. In Auer and Di Luzio (eds) *Interpretative Sociolinguistics: Migrants – Children – Migrant Children*. Tübingen, Gunter Narr Verlag.

Auer J C P and Di Luzio A 1983a On structure and meaning of linguistic variation in Italian migrant children in Germany. In Bäuerle R, Schwarze Ch, Stechow A V, (eds) *Meaning, Use and Interpretation of Language*. Berlin, De Gruyter pp. 1–21.

Auer J C P and Di Luzio A 1983b Three types of variation and their interpretation. In L. Dabene, M. Flasaquier and J. Lyons (eds) *Status of Migrants' 'Mother Tongues'/ Le Statut des Langues D'origine des Migrants*. Strasbourg, European Science Foundation pp. 67–100.

Auer J C P and Di Luzio A (eds) 1984 *Interpretive Sociolinguistics: Migrants – Children – Migrant Children*. Tuebingen, Gunter Narr Verlag.

Bailey B L 1966 *Jamaican Creole Syntax: a Transformational Approach*. Cambridge, Cambridge University Press.

Bailey B L 1971 Can dialect boundaries be defined? In Hymes D (ed) *Pidginization and Creolization*, 341–8. Cambridge, Cambridge University Press.

Bailey C J N 1973 *Variation and Linguistic Theory*. Washington, DC, Center for Applied Linguistics.

Beaken M A 1971 *A Study of Phonological Development in a Primary School Population of East London*. PhD thesis, University of London.

Beebe L M 1981 Social and situational factors affecting the communicative strategy of dialect code-switching. *International Journal of the Sociology of Language* 32: 139–49.

Bell A 1984 Language style as audience design. *Language in Society* 13: 145–204.

Bickerton D 1973 On the nature of a creole continuum. *Language* 49: 641–69.

Bickerton D 1975 *Dynamics of a Creole System*. Cambridge, Cambridge University Press.

Blom J P and Gumperz J J 1972 Social meaning in linguistic structures. In Gumperz J J, Hymes D (eds) *Directions in Sociolinguistics*. New York, Holt, Rinehart and Winston.

Bones J 1986a Language and Rastafari. In Sutcliffe D and Wong A (eds) *The Language of the Black Experience*. Oxford, Blackwell, pp. 37–51.

Bones J 1986b Reggae Deejaying and Jamaican Afro-Lingua. In Sutcliffe D and Wong A (eds) *The Language of the Black Experience*. Oxford, Blackwell, pp. 52–68.

Bullock A 1975 *A Language for Life*. London, HMSO.

Carrington L 1984 *St Lucian Creole: a Descriptive Analysis of its Phonology and Morpho-syntax*, Kreolische Bibliothek, Volume 6. Hamburg, Buske.

Cassidy F G 1961 *Jamaica Talk: Three Hundred Years of the English Language in Jamaica*. London, Macmillan.

Cassidy F G, Le Page R B 1967, 1980 *Dictionary of Jamaican English*. 2nd edn. Cambridge, Cambridge University Press.

Coupland N 1984 Accommodation at work: some phonological data and their implications. *International Journal of the Sociology of Language* 46: 49–70.

Crump S 1979 *The Language of West Indian Children and its Relevance for Schools*. Unpublished MA dissertation, University of London Institute of Education. Not available for loan. (Reference in Edwards V 1986 Language in a black community *Multilingual Matters*, 24: 31)

Dalphinis M 1991 The Afro-English creole speech community. In Alladina and Edwards (eds), *Multilingualism in the British Isles Volume 2: Africa and The Middle East and Asia*. London, Longman, pp. 42–56.

D'Costa J 1981 Review of Edwards 1979. *Harvard Educational Review* 51: 193–7.

De Camp D 1971 Towards a generative analysis of a post-creole speech continuum. In Hymes D (ed) *Pidginization and Creolization of Languages: Proceedings of a Conference held at The University of the West Indies, Mona, Jamaica, April 1968*. Cambridge, Cambridge University Press, pp. 349–70.

Di Sciullo A, Muysken P, Singh R 1986 Government and Code-mixing. *Journal of Linguistics* 22: 1–24.

Edwards V 1979 *The West Indian Language Issue in British Schools: Challenges and Responses*. London, Routledge and Kegan Paul.

Edwards V 1982 Research priorities in the study of Black British English. Mimeo. Unpublished. Reading, Bulmershe College of Higher Education.

Edwards V 1986 *Language in a Black Community*. Clevedon (Avon), Multilingual Matters Ltd.

Fairclough N L 1992 *Critical Language Awareness*. Harlow, Longman.

Ferguson C A 1959 Diglossia. *Word* 15: 325–40.

Fishman J 1965 Who speaks what language to whom and when? *Linguistique* 2: 57–88.

Fishman J 1967 Bilingualism with and without diglossia: Diglossia with and without bilingualism. *Journal of Social Issues* 23: 29–38.

Fishman J 1980 Bilingualism and biculturalism as individual and as societal phenomena. *Journal of Multilingual and Multicultural Development* **1**: 3–16.

Garfinkel H 1974 On the origins of the term 'ethnomethodology'. In Turner R (ed) *Ethnomethodology*. Harmondsworth, Penguin.

Gibson K A 1982 Tense and Aspect in Guyanese Creole: a syntactic, semantic and pragmatic analysis. Unpublished D Phil. dissertation, University of York.

Giles H, Powesland P F 1975 *Speech Style and Social Evaluation*. London, Academic Press.

Giles H, Smith P 1979 Accommodation theory: optimal levels of convergence. In Giles H, St Clair R N (eds) *Language and Social Psychology*. Oxford, Blackwell.

Gilroy P 1987 *There Ain't No Black in the Union Jack*. London, Hutchinson.

Goffman E 1981 *Forms of Talk*. Oxford, Basil Blackwell.

Griffith J A G, Henderson J, Wood D 1960 *Coloured Immigrants in Britain*. Oxford, Institute of Race Relations and Oxford University Press.

Gumperz J J 1971 Dialect differences and social stratification in a North Indian village. In Gumperz J J (ed) *Language in Social Groups*. Stanford, Stanford University Press.

Gumperz J J 1982 *Discourse Strategies*. Cambridge, Cambridge University Press.

Harris J 1984 Syntactic variation and dialect divergence. *Journal of Linguistics* **20**: 303–27.

Henderson J 1960 A sociological report. In Griffith J A G et al. *Coloured Immigrants in Britain*, Oxford, Institute of Race Relations and Oxford University Press.

Heritage J 1984 *Garfinkel* and *Ethnomethodology*. Cambridge, Polity Press.

Hewitt R 1982 White adolescent Creole users and the politics of friendship. *Journal of Multilingual and Multicultural Development* **3** (3): 217–32.

Hewitt R 1986 *White Talk Black Talk*. Cambridge, Cambridge University Press.

Hewitt R 1989 Creole in the Classroom: political grammars and educational vocabularies. In Grillo R (ed) *Social Anthropology and the Politics of Language*. London, Routledge.

Holm J A (ed) 1983 *Central American English. Varieties of English Around the World, Volume T2*. Heidelberg, Julius Groos Verlag.

Holm J A 1989 *Pidgins and Creoles*. Cambridge, Cambridge University Press.

Hymes D (ed) 1971 *Pidginization and Creolization of Languages: Proceedings of a Conference Held at the University of the West Indies, Mona, Jamaica, April 1968*. Cambridge, Cambridge University Press.

Inner London Education Authority (ILEA) Afro-Caribbean Language and Literacy Project 1990 *Language and Power: Language Materials for Students in the Multilingual and Multiethnic classroom*. London, Harcourt Brace Jovanovitch.

Joshi A K 1985 Processing of sentences with intrasentential code-switching. In Dowty D, Karttunen L, Zwicky A (eds), *Natural Language Processing: Psychological, Computational and Theoretical Perspectives*. Cambridge, Cambridge University Press.

Khan F 1991 The Urdu speech community. In Alladina S and Edwards V (eds) *Multilingualism in the British Isles, Volume 2: Africa, The Middle East and Asia*. Harlow, Longman.

Kingman J 1988 *Report of the Committee of Inquiry into the English Language*. London, HMSO.

Labov W 1966 *The Social Stratification of English in New York City*. Washington, DC, Center for Applied Linguistics.

Lambert W E, Hodgson R C, Gardner R C, Fillenbaum S 1960 Evaluational reactions to spoken language. *Journal of Abnormal and Social Psychology* 60: 44–51.

Lavandera B R 1978 Where does the sociolinguistic variable stop? *Language in Society* 7: 171–82.

Laver J 1991 *The Gift of Speech: Papers in the Analysis of Speech and Voice*. Edinburgh University Press.

Lawton D 1980 Language attitude, Discreteness and Code Shifting in Jamaican Creole. *English World Wide* 1(2): 221–6.

Le Page R B 1961 (ed) *Creole Language Studies 2: Proceedings of the Conference on Creole Language Studies, 1959*. London, Macmillan.

Le Page R B 1980 Projection, Focussing, Diffusion. *York Papers in Linguistics, 9*.

Le Page R B 1981 *Caribbean Connections in the Classroom*. London, Mary Glasgow Language Trust.

Le Page R B, De Camp D 1960 *Creole Language Studies 1: Jamaican Creole*. London, Macmillan.

Le Page R B, Tabouret-Keller A 1985 *Acts of Identity: Creole-based Approaches to Language and Ethnicity*. Cambridge, Cambridge University Press.

Lenneberg E 1967 *The Biological Foundations of Language*. New York, John Wiley and Sons.

Levinson S C 1983 *Pragmatics*. Cambridge, Cambridge University Press.

Local J K, Wells W H G, Sebba M 1985 Phonology for conversation: phonetic aspects of turn delimitation in London Jamaican. *Journal of Pragmatics* 9(2): 309–30.

Martin-Jones M 1991 Sociolinguistic surveys as a source of evidence in the study of bilingualism: a critical assessment of survey work conducted among linguistic minorities in three British cities. In K. de Bot and W. Fase (eds) *Migrant Languages in Western Europe. International Journal of the Sociology of Language* 90: 37–55.

Milroy L 1980 *Language and Social Networks*. Oxford, Blackwell.

Milroy J, Milroy L (eds) 1993 *Real English: the Grammar of English Dialects in the British Isles*. Harlow, Longman.

Milroy L, Li Wei (forthcoming) Language Choice and Social Networks in the Tyneside Community: Developing an Explanatory Model. In Lüdi D, Milroy L, Muysken P (eds) *One Speaker: Two Languages: Cross Disciplinary Perspectives on Code Switching*. European Science Foundation.

Mühlhäusler P 1986 *Pidgin and Creole Linguistics*. Oxford, Blackwell.

Mungo C 1979 The use of a dialect of West Indian origin in British schools. *Education Journal* 2(1): 2–4.

Myers-Scotton C 1992 The matrix frame model: a production-based view of codeswitching. Prepared for volume on code switching sponsored by European Science Foundation. MS.

Nordenstam K 1979 *Svenskan i Norge*. Gothenburg, University Press.

Nwenmely H 1991 The Kwéyòl Speech Community. In Alladina S and Edwards V (eds) *Multilingualism in the British Isles, Volume 2: Africa, The Middle East and Asia*. Harlow, Longman.

Pardoe S 1992 Review of: Inner London Education Authority Afro-Caribbean Language and Literacy Project (1990). *Language Issues* 5: 1, 35–36 (Autumn/Winter 1991/92)

Pollard V 1980 Dread talk: the speech of the Rastafarians in Jamaica. *Caribbean Quarterly* 26: 32–41.

Pollard V 1983 The social history of dread talk. In Carrington L D (ed), *Studies in Caribbean Language*. St Augustine, Trinidad: Society for Caribbean Linguistics, pp. 46–62.

Pollard V 1984a Word sounds: the language of Rastafari in Barbados and St Lucia. *Jamaica Journal* 17: 57–62.

Pollard V 1984b Rastafarian language in St Lucia and Barbados. In Sebba M and Todd L (eds) *Papers from the York Creole Conference*. York Papers in Linguistics 11.

Pomerantz A M 1975 Second assessments: a study of some features of agreements/disagreements. PhD thesis. University of California, Irvine.

Pomerantz A M 1984 Agreeing and disagreeing with assessments: some features of preferred/dispreferred turn shapes. In Atkinson J M and Heritage J (eds) *Structures of Social Action: Studies in Conversation Analysis*. Cambridge, Cambridge University Press.

Poplack S 1980 Sometimes I'll start a sentence in Spanish Y TERMINO EN ESPAÑOL: towards a typology of code-switching. *Linguistics* 7/8: 581–618.

Rampton A 1981 *West Indian Children in Our Schools* (Interim report of the Committee of Inquiry into the Education of Children from Ethnic Minority Groups). London, HMSO.

Rogers I 1981 The influence of Australian English intonation on the speech of two British children. *Working papers of the Speech and Language Research Centre, Macquarie University* 3: 25–42.

Romaine S 1982 *Socio-historical Linguistics: its Status and Methodology*. Cambridge, Cambridge University Press.

Romaine S 1984 *The Language of Children and Adolescents: the Acquisition of Communicative Competence*. Oxford, Basil Blackwell.

Romaine S 1988 *Pidgin and Creole Languages*. Harlow, Longman.

Romaine S 1989 *Bilingualism*. Oxford, Basil Blackwell.

Rosen H, Burgess T 1980 *Languages and Dialects of London School Children*. London, Ward Lock Educational.

Ryan S 1980 *Rastafarianism and the Speech of Adolescent Blacks in Britain*. Unpublished MA thesis, Department of English, University of Birmingham.

Sacks H, Schegloff E, Jefferson G 1978 A simplest systematics for the organization of turn-taking in conversation. In Schenkein J (ed) *Studies in the Organization of Conversational Interaction.* New York, Academic Press.

Schools Council 1972 *Teaching English to West Indian Children, Concept 7–9.* London, Edward Arnold.

Sebba M, Tate S 1986 You know what I mean? Agreement marking in British Black English. *Journal of Pragmatics* 10.

Sebba M, Wootton A J 1984 Conversational code-switching in London Jamaican. Paper presented at Sociolinguistics Symposium 5, Liverpool.

Simon D 1982 *Railton Blues.* London, Bogle-L'Ouverture.

Sivertsen E 1960 *Cockney Phonology.* Oslo University Press.

Stone M 1981 *The Education of the Black Child in Britain: the Myth of Multicultural Education.* London, Fontana.

Sutcliffe D 1982a *British Black English.* Oxford, Blackwell.

Sutcliffe D 1982b *Black British Narrative Patterns.* Report to the ESRC.

Sutcliffe D and Wong A (eds) 1986 *The Language of the Black Experience.* Oxford, Blackwell.

Tate S 1984 Jamaican Creole Approximation by Second-Generation Dominicans?: The use of Agreement Tokens. Unpublished MA thesis, Department of Language and Linguistics, University of York.

Taylor T J, Cameron D 1987 *Analysing Conversation: Rules and Units in the Structure of Talk.* Oxford, Pergamon Press.

Thakerar J N, Giles H, Cheshire J 1982 Psychological and linguistic parameters of speech accommodation theory. In Fraser C and Scherer K R (eds) *Advances in the Social Psychology of Language.* Cambridge University Press, pp. 205–55.

Todd L 1990 *Pidgins and Creoles* (2nd edn). London, Routledge.

Trudgill P 1974 *The Social Differentiation of English in Norwich.* London, Cambridge University Press.

Trudgill P 1982 Linguistic accommodation: sociolinguistic observations on a sociopsychological theory. In Fretheim T and Hellan L (eds) *Sixth Scandinavian Conference of Linguistics.* Trondheim, Tapir.

Trudgill P 1986 *Dialects in Contact.* Oxford, Basil Blackwell.

Wells J C 1973 *Jamaican Pronunciation in London.* Oxford, Basil Blackwell.

Wells J C 1982 *Accents of English*. Cambridge, Cambridge University Press.

Wight J 1971 Dialect in School. *Educational Review* 24(1): 47–58.

Wood D. 1960 A general survey. In Griffith J A G et al. *Coloured Immigrants in Britain*, Oxford, Institute of Race Relations and Oxford University Press.

Wootton A J 1981 The management of grantings and rejections by parents in request sequences. *Semiotica* 37: 59–89.

Wootton A J and Sebba M 1984 Conversational code-switching in London Jamaican. Paper presented to Sociolinguistics Symposium 5, Liverpool.

Wright F J 1984 A sociolinguistic study of passivization amongst black adolescents in Britain. Unpublished PhD thesis, Department of Linguistics, University of Birmingham.

Index